J. M. SYNGE

The Playboy of the Western World

With Commentary and Notes by
NON WORRALL

Methuen Student Editions
METHUEN · DRAMA

This Methuen Student Edition first published in 1983 by Methuen
London Ltd
Reprinted 1986

Reprinted 1990 by Methuen Drama,
Michelin House, 81 Fulham Road, London SW3 6RB
Reprinted 1991

ISBN 0 413 51940 6

Printed in Great Britain by Cox & Wyman Ltd, Reading

Contents

John Millington Synge: 1871-1909

1871 16 April. Edmund John Millington Synge, the youngest of five children, born at Newtown Villas, Rathfarnham, near Dublin.

1872 Synge's father, a barrister, died of smallpox. The family moved to Rathgar, two miles nearer to Dublin, living conservatively but in a style befitting their class. Synge was greatly affected by the atmosphere of religious intensity generated by his mother, the daughter of a Protestant rector. Synge's health was always poor. Asthma necessitated private tuition at home. From an early age he showed an interest in nature and studied ornithology, making many excursions into the surrounding countryside. Summer vacations were usually spent at Greystones, a small fishing village in County Wicklow on the south east coast.

1885 He read Darwin and suffered a crisis of faith. He began to move away from his family's religion towards agnosticism which further increased the sense of isolation which was to mark his whole life. There were fierce family arguments because his brother Edward, as land agent of the family estates in Wicklow, had evicted tenants for non-payment of rent. Synge was opposed to his brother's actions and methods but his mother supported them.

1887 Music began to figure importantly in his life when he started studying the violin.

1888- -92 Under pressure from his mother, Synge unwillingly attended Trinity College, Dublin but was a poor student, making little effort and finally being awarded a pass degree — the lowest category to be given. While at university, he became interested in Irish antiquities and began reading Irish patriotic literature as well as studying Hebrew and Gaelic. Despite his mother's opposition to what she considered a frivolous activity, Synge continued his music studies, being awarded a scholarship to study at the Royal Irish Academy of Music in December 1891.

1892 Synge began to write poetry very much in the style of

Wordsworth. He fell in love with Cherry Matheson, the daughter of an intensely religious (Plymouth Brethren) family, new neighbours in Crossthwaite Park, Kingstown, a fashionable metropolitan suburb of Dublin to which the Synges had moved two years previously.

1893   Mary Synge, cousin and concert pianist, persuaded Synge's mother to allow Synge to go to Germany to continue his music studies. He spent a large part of each of the next seven years abroad. Although not rich, he was wealthy enough not to have any real financial worries.

1894-   Visits to Germany to study music, to Paris to study French
96   at the Sorbonne, and to Italy. In what was to prove to be the first in a series of unhappy love affairs, he proposed to Cherry Matheson without success and then wrote *Vita Vecchia,* a sequence of poems linked by prose narrative, the subject being a perfunctorily disguised version of his affair with Cherry. In Paris he met Dr. James Cree, an Irish Nationalist, who introduced him to W.B. Yeats and Maud Gonne. He began reading socialist literature including Marx and William Morris.

1897   Synge joined the Irish League but resigned after three months. He read Yeats and showed a growing interest in the work of enthusiasts who were trying to preserve continental vestiges of Celtic civilization. He began *Étude Morbide* which was written in the form of a violinist's diary, the subject matter utilizing Synge's doubts of his own musical abilities, his thoughts upon religious truth, his appreciation of peasant life in Brittany and his difficulties with girl friends. He underwent an operation in Dublin to remove lumps which had developed on the side of his neck, the first signs of cancer of the lymphatic glands. His hair also fell out.

1898   Back in Paris, wearing a distinctive black wig and soft felt hat, he sketched rough drafts of possible plays.

May: Prompted by an earlier suggestion from Yeats, Synge paid his first visit to the Aran Islands off the west coast of Ireland. He took photographs and made notes on the way of life and language of the islanders.

27 June: Crucial first meeting with Lady Gregory and Edward Martyn who were planning, along with Yeats, to produce Celtic and Irish plays in Dublin.

1899-   Synge's time was divided between Dublin and Paris. On
1901   holiday each year in the Aran Islands, he was gradually

collecting material for a book on the islands. He worked at preliminary sketches and dialogue for *Riders to the Sea*. Encouraged by Lady Gregory, Synge left the manuscript of *The Aran Islands* with the London publisher, Grant Richards, but it was rejected. Synge became extremely downcast — at the age of thirty he had published only six articles, two of which were book reviews. He refused an operation on the worsening swelling on his neck from which he had no pain, although he was embarrassed by its unsightliness.

1902   Two more of Synge's articles were published in *L'Européen*, one on mediaeval Celtic literature and the other on the intellectual movement in Ireland, dealing with the slow development over two centuries of a proper Irish literature. After relatively unsuccessful attempts at two verse plays, only fragments of which have survived, he wrote *In the Shadow of the Glen* and *Riders to the Sea* which he gave to Lady Gregory for performance by the Fays. He also produced the first draft of *The Tinker's Wedding* which was later re-written and enlarged to two acts. His essay *The Old and the New in Ireland* dealt with the whole problem of Gaelic language revival and the creation of a modern Irish literature based upon native tradition.

1903   Synge tried without success to get London publishers interested in his work. In Paris he met James Joyce with whom he had many 'friendly' arguments. He started work on *The Well of the Saints* which centres upon two blind beggars who have their sight miraculously restored by a saint but their happiness as man and wife destroyed. Synge spent the summer in West Kerry where he noted that although the people were bilingual, a colourful English was usually dominant.

8 October: First performance of *In the Shadow of the Glen*. Only one of the five main Dublin newspapers gave a favourable review to this one-act play dealing with a jealous husband who feigns death to test the fidelity of his wife. Here began the hostile public reception of Synge's work.

1904   25 February: First performance of *Riders to the Sea,* a one-act play set in an island fishing community, centring on a mother's loss of the last two of several sons to the sea. The audience was small but enthusiastic, the press reception cool.

26 March: London performances of *Riders to the Sea* and *In the Shadow of the Glen* by the Fay company at the Royalty Theatre were highly praised. Synge was closely involved with Yeats and Lady Gregory over the establishing of a new theatre to be financed by Miss Annie Horniman. He spent August in Kerry and in September visited Northern Mayo including the Mullet peninsula.

1905   Articles on Aran life published in *The Manchester Guardian* which then commissioned Synge with Jack Yeats, painter brother of the poet, to do a series of illustrated articles on life in the Congested Districts — poverty stricken areas of Galway so designated because it was a wilderness lacking the fertility to support its rather heavy population.

September: Synge became, with Yeats and Lady Gregory, one of the three directors of the reorganized Irish National Theatre Society. The only one of the three resident in Dublin, Synge began to play a far more active role in the management of the theatre.

December: Molly Allgood joined the company and Synge rapidly fell in love with her. Beset by differences in age (she was fourteen years younger than Synge), religion (she was Roman Catholic) and background (she was a working-class girl who had little education), their relationship was always stormy.

1906   Synge began the first draft of *Playboy*, at this point called *Murder Will Out*. In the summer he became secretly engaged to Molly, but his state of health was beginning to worry him.

1907   Rehearsals began for *Playboy* with Molly as Pegeen Mike.

26 January: The now notorious first night of *Playboy*.

February: Maunsel & Co. (Dublin) published the play; two hundred copies sold in the first week.

May: Abbey Company toured England; *Playboy* was a great success in Oxford and London and in the same month Maunsel & Co. published *The Aran Islands*.

October: Synge began work on *Deirdre of the Sorrows*, a play based on Irish mythology. Interrupted by his worsening health. His marriage was postponed until the glands in his neck had been removed, which was apparently done successfully, but by December Synge felt increasing pain from what proved to be a tumour in his side.

1908   Exploratory surgery revealed the size and nature of the tumour but the extent of his illness was kept secret from Synge. In October his poems were accepted for publication by both the Cuala Press and Maunsel & Co. He went to Germany on holiday but was recalled by a telegram announcing his mother's death. Synge desperately wanted to finish *Deirdre* but, even with Molly's help, as his health gradually worsened, this became impossible. (After his death, the 'final' version of *Deirdre* was assembled from Synge's manuscripts by Yeats, Lady Gregory and Molly.)

1909 February: He returned to the Elpis Nursing Home in Dublin but doctors decided not to operate.

24 March: Synge died, aged 37. He was buried in the family plot in Mount Jerome Cemetery, Dublin, after a brief service at the graveside.

Left to right: Maire O'Neill (real name: Molly Allgood, Synge's fiancée) as Pegeen, Arthur Sinclair (later Maire O'Neill's husband) as Michael, and Fred O'Donovan as Christy in a 1921 production at the Royal Court Theatre, London. (Photo: Mander & Mitchenson)

Introduction

Plot

The entire action of the play takes place in a wayside bar owned by Michael James Flaherty on a road near a village on the wild coast of County Mayo in Western Ireland.

Act One

It is an autumn evening and dusk is falling. The play opens with Pegeen Mike, Michael's twenty-year-old daughter, listing the items of her trousseau to be ordered in connection with her forthcoming marriage to her timid cousin, Shawn Keogh. When Shawn himself enters and asks where Michael James is, she reveals that her father intends to go off to a funeral wake with some of his friends, leaving Pegeen on her own throughout the dark night. Shawn suggests fetching the Widow Quin to keep Pegeen company — he makes the excuse that he cannot stay with her himself since this might offend the parish priest — and tells her of the groaning noises he has heard coming from a nearby ditch. He pleads with Pegeen not to tell her father and the other men about his fear of what or who is in the ditch for he knows they will make it a subject of laughter and gossip at the wake. Pegeen deliberately leaves him in doubt as to what she intends to do as her father enters, accompanied by two local farmers, Philly Cullen and Jimmy Farrell.

Michael refuses to heed his daughter's complaints about being left alone except to try jokingly to force Shawn to stay and keep her company. To their amusement Shawn runs off in fright but returns almost immediately having been even more terrified by the sight of the man appearing out of the ditch

Enter Christy Mahon, a slight young man, very tired, frightened and dirty. By a cautious process of question and answer, the men tempt Christy into revealing that he has killed his father by hitting him on the head with a spade he was using for digging potatoes. The men, instead of being afraid or reporting him to the police, are impressed and, despite Shawn's protestations, Michael accepts Pegeen's suggestion, offering Christy refuge and employment as pot-boy in the bar. Michael and his friends leave; Shawn now attempts to stay with Pegeen but she throws him out.

On his own with Pegeen, Christy, encouraged by the reception of his story, describes the quiet undistinguished life he has led in the North. She is disappointed that this picture is hardly that of a rebellious murderer, but an obvious sympathy is evident between them. Their conversation is interrupted by the arrival of the Widow Quin (aged about thirty) who says she's been sent by Shawn Keogh and Father Reilly to take Christy off to lodge with her. We discover that Widow Quin too is guilty of a murder — that of her husband — which is described by Pegeen in deliberately inglorious terms. The two women exchange insults and invective, each trying to prove the other unworthy of Christy's companionship. Christy decides in favour of Pegeen and the Widow is forced to retire, her parting shot being a reference to Pegeen's engagement. When questioned about this by Christy, Pegeen is adamant that she has no intention of marrying Shawn. As she leaves to fetch Christy some bedding, the act concludes with Christy delighting in his new situation and wishing he'd killed his father years before.

Act Two

It is the next morning. Christy, counting the glasses on the bar while cleaning Pegeen's boots, soliloquises on the advantages of living this new life forever. Inspecting his face in a looking-glass, he contemplates how fine a man he now is. Hearing and seeing strange girls approach, he rushes in panic, still holding the mirror, into an inner room.

The Village Girls, Susan Brady, Honor Blake and Sara Tansey, enter obviously intent upon seeing for themselves the stranger who has killed his father and of whom they have already heard so much in the village. Discovering Christy, they present him with gifts brought in admiration of his deed. Widow Quin arrives and encourages the girls to make tea and get Christy's breakfast. Christy, gaining in confidence, enlarges further, in terms reminiscent of the Irish sagas, on the story of how he killed his father. Sara, deciding he would make an ideal husband for the Widow, pours them a glass of beer each which they are about to drink with arms linked when Pegeen enters.

In face of Pegeen's jealous anger, the girls quickly make up excuses for their presence but are thrown out by Pegeen, as is the Widow. Left alone with Christy, Pegeen, in retaliation for his flirting with the girls, treats him scornfully and seeks to intimidate his male assurance with graphic descriptions of the kind of hanging which a murderer like him can expect. Christy decides he must leave but at this point Pegeen calls him to her, reminding him of his position as pot-boy and revealing that he is in no danger since she has discovered that so far there has been no public report of his father's murder. Realising that she was only making fun of him, Christy is delighted to be able to stay with Pegeen.

Shawn Keogh and the Widow Quin run in with news that Pegeen's father's sheep have broken into a cabbage field. Pegeen rushes off to deal with this emergency but Christy is prevented from following her. Shawn, supported by the Widow, tries to bribe Christy to leave with the offer of a one-way ticket to America as well as Shawn's new hat, breeches and coat. Christy goes into the inner room to try on the clothes. Widow Quin proceeds to suggest that she marry Christy, and Shawn willingly agrees to all the material goods and rights she requests in order to have her support in removing Christy as a rival for the hand of Pegeen. When Christy re-enters wearing Shawn's smart clothes, Shawn tactfully leaves him alone with the Widow.

Christy is swaggering around boasting when he glances out of the window and sees his 'dead' father passing by with his head heavily bandaged. Old Mahon enters and Christy hides behind the door. In response to the Widow's probing, Old Mahon recounts his own version of his son's attack upon him. The Widow tells him that she saw someone resembling his son on his way to catch the steamer and gives Old Mahon directions to follow. When he has gone she mocks Christy's former boasting to the point where he weeps in despair at the thought of Pegeen's reaction to the changed situation and the probability of losing her. The Widow cunningly now makes her offer of marriage but in the face of Christy's love for Pegeen accepts instead the bargain of keeping Old Mahon's 'resurrection' secret in return for the same grazing and other rights she had demanded from Shawn. They also plan to proclaim Old Mahon a maniac should he appear again and recognise Christy.

The girls return and run off with Christy to the sports on the sands.

Act Three
Later the same day Jimmy and Philly, slightly drunk from their celebrations at the wake, enter. They have sent Shawn to collect Michael in the donkey cart. Annoyed that all the drink is locked away, Philly contrasts Pegeen's neglect of her customers with her fussing over Christy but Jimmy finds her interest quite understandable since Christy is winning all the games of chance as

well as the various sports. As they are talking, Old Mahon appears, disappointed in the search, and joins in their macabre conversation about skeletons by drawing attention to the uniquely splintered state of his own skull. Having caught their interest, he begs for a drink in return for which he promises to tell them his story.

Widow Quin then enters and stands aghast at the sight of Old Mahon. She gives him the drink he begs for and, taking Jimmy and Philly to one side, pursues the plan already devised with Christy of declaring Old Mahon to be a lunatic. However, when Mahon talks, it is apparent to Philly that he is not the madman the Widow claims him to be. Attention is diverted by the noise of the donkey race which is about to be run. The Widow fails in her attempt to hurry Mahon off as Philly encourages him to stay and watch the race with them from the inn window.

Details of the events of the race are conveyed to the audience by the reactions of the four observers. As the race is won by Christy and he is carried shoulder high towards the pub, Old Mahon recognises his son. The Widow prevents Mahon from rushing out to confront Christy and persuades him that he is mad to think that such a celebrated victor could be the son he had earlier described as a daydreamer and ne'er-do-well. Rather than risk being treated cruelly as a local maniac, Mahon sees the wisdom of a hasty retreat. Philly suspects the Widow of scheming so decides to follow him. Jimmy follows Philly but he is fully convinced by the Widow's story and gleefully anticipates his friend being attacked by the madman.

The crowd rush in bearing Christy and his trophies in triumph, shouting their congratulations. Accepting their applause and gifts, Christy observes that these achievements are small compared with what he once accomplished with a single blow of a spade. As the town crier is heard announcing the tug-o'-war, Pegeen hustles everybody out so that she is left alone with the conqueror.

Christy, encouraged by Pegeen's delight and pride in his achievements, asks her to marry him in a fortnight's time. Pegeen at first backs away, suggesting that in a few months Christy will return home and pursue some other girl. Thus provoked, Christy pours forth his love for Pegeen with such rapture and tenderness that she, to her own surprise, responds in similar tones.

Their lovemaking is interrupted by the drunken singing of Michael returning from the wake. Pegeen decides to tell him of their intentions once he has slept and sobered up. When Michael enters, held up by Shawn, he scolds Christy for not having given his murdered father a decent burial with the wake which would be a necessary, celebratory, part of the ritual. Boasting of the qualities of his future son-in-law, he informs them that the dispensation allowing Pegeen and Shawn to marry has arrived. Pegeen announces that she now intends to marry Christy, dismissing her father's objections to having a murderer as a son-in-law by contrasting Christy's manly 'savagery' and fine words with Shawn's puny 'scarecrow' nature. When Michael tries to force Shawn to fight Christy, Shawn flies out of the door in terror. Michael then joins the hands of Pegeen and Christy, accepting their forthcoming union with his blessing.

A hubbub outside erupts on to the stage as Old Mahon rushes in pursued by the crowd and Widow Quin. He knocks Christy down and proceeds to beat him. When he reveals his identity to Pegeen she immediately rounds on Christy in bitter disillusion, calling him a liar and telling Mahon to take his son away. Provoked by this humiliation, Christy takes up a spade, runs at his father and chases him out of the door, followed by everybody else. There is a great noise outside, then a yell followed by a momentary dead silence. It would seem that Christy has succeeded this time where he failed before.

Christy re-enters alone and goes to the fire. The Widow rushes in, urging him to leave since the crowd, appalled by the reality of the deed, have turned against him and he is likely to be hanged but Christy is convinced that now Pegeen will once more praise him. Sara Tansey runs in, offering Christy one of her petticoats to disguise himself so that he can run away from the villagers. As the two women try to fasten the petticoat on him, Christy threatens them with a stool. They leave with the idea of saving him from the gallows by fetching a doctor to declare him insane. Christy is left alone by the fire.

The men crowd in the doorway, discussing at this safe distance how to get the rope around the murderer's neck. Pegeen takes the lead and the noose is dropped over Christy's shoulders and pulled tight around his arms. Christy questions why Pegeen is treating him like this instead of praising him. As the men pull on the rope, Christy pleads in terror for Pegeen to cut his bonds. She refuses, encouraging the men to haul him away to the police. In an effort to escape, Christy squirms round on the floor and bites Shawn's leg. At this, Pegeen, who at Shawn's instigation has been using the bellows on the fire to generate as much heat as possible, brings a lighted sod of turf over and viciously burns Christy's leg.

As they are dragging Christy towards the door, Jimmy suddenly notices Old Mahon who, still alive, has crawled in moments previously. They all drop Christy and scatter in fear. Christy confronts his father on all fours. At first the old man automatically tries to take charge and attempts to lead Christy away. However, to his father's delight, the son declares himself master and they go off together, Christy envisaging a nomadic life of romantic storytelling.

Michael welcomes the return of peace and instructs Pegeen to serve beer. Shawn attempts to re-establish his relationship with her but Pegeen boxes his ears and breaks out into wild lamentations of grief as the realisation dawns on her: she has lost 'the only Playboy of the Western World.'

The cast of the 1976 National Theatre production, London: *Back row:* Bellman (Harry Webster), Philly (P.G. Stephens), Shawn (Jim Norton), Jimmy (Eddie Byrne), Peasants (Kevin Flood and Michael Keating); *Middle Row:* Old Mahon (J.G. Devlin), Pegeen (Susan Fleetwood), Christy (Stephen Rea), Widow Quin (Margaret Whiting), Michael (Liam Redmond); *Front row:* Village girls (Terry Donnelly, Jeananne Crowley, Nora Connolly). (Photo: Haynes)

Synge's Ireland

Social and political conditions

Although the Ireland of Synge's day was not yet divided into
Northern Ireland and Eire — the Partition of Ireland being effected
in 1920 by the Government of Ireland Act — it could hardly be
described as a country at peace with itself.

By birth, Synge belonged to what was called the Anglo-Irish
Ascendancy. His Protestant family was middle-class, professional
and land-owning, though based on Dublin. They supported the rule
of the English crown over a people the majority of whom were
Catholic peasants.

Crucial events which shaped the Ireland of the later nineteenth
century were as follows:

From the early seventeenth century onwards, a mixture of city
company representatives from London and lowland Scots began to
settle in Ulster, the northernmost region of the four divisions of
Ireland. These were the ancestors of the 'Orangemen'.

With the triumph of Oliver Cromwell over Charles I, the
persecution of, and discrimination against, Irish Catholics who had
supported Charles began. It intensified after the defeat of James II
at the Battle of the Boyne in 1689 which secured the throne of
England for the Protestant William of Orange (William III). The
Catholic Emancipation Bill, which at least in part reversed this
process, was not passed until 1829 after intense pressure by the
Catholic Association founded in 1823 by Daniel O'Connell.

During the eighteenth century, there were attempts to unite the
Irish, regardless of religious differences, against the English to rid
the country of what had become in effect English colonial rule.
With the capture and death of Wolfe Tone, the leader of the
Society of United Irishmen, this opposition collapsed so that it was
possible for William Pitt to dissolve the Irish parliament in 1800
and pronounce formal union with Britain. This inevitably had the
effect of intensifying the split in allegiance within the nation so
that by the second half of the nineteenth century, it became more
and more difficult even to sympathise with 'the other side': the
Protestants were virtually unanimous in their support for the
Union whilst nearly all Catholics called for Home Rule so that the

Irish could govern themselves. This question was one of the two vital political concerns of Synge's time. Only four years before he was born, the Fenian Rising had occurred, the failure of which was to affect the reception of *Playboy* in the United States, since the Fenians, whose ancestors had emigrated to New York, figured significantly in the uproar which greeted the first performance.

The other crucial concern in Synge's Ireland, and one more obviously reflected in his work, was the question of Land Reform. Although less significant in the more industrialised north (Ulster), the larger, agrarian portion of Ireland was suffering intensely from the evils of absentee landlordism, high rents and a lack of security of land tenure. A peasant population whose life was often conducted at little above subsistence level formed the majority of the nation, a lifestyle far removed from that of more privileged families like the Synges.

Conditions in the countryside were further worsened by the Potato Famine which deprived the peasant families of their staple diet. As a result, between 1846 and 1851, the population shrank from 8 to 6½ million, half of the 2½ million having died, the other half having emigrated to the United States or to England where they became labourers. The Government failed to offer any form of relief; and, instead of trying to help their tenants, some landlords merely embarked upon a policy of evicting the increasing number who could no longer pay their rent. The brutal methods, involving battering rams and the wrecking of cottages, enraged more than the working class. It was this which led to the emergence of Charles Stuart Parnell, the 'uncrowned king of Ireland', who 'betrayed' his own Protestant land-owning class when he sided with the down-trodden peasants. Parnell and his followers fought the authorities during Synge's lifetime, even after Parnell was discredited and lost the support of Gladstone and the Liberal Party by being cited in the famous O'Shea divorce case.

Synge's own attitude towards the 'Land Problem' can be seen in his opposition to his own brother's eviction of tenants but it is important to realise that he remained capable of seeing what was valuable and worth retaining in the culture of the ruling class. He was moved by the tragedy of both sides in the battle for Ireland:

The broken greenhouses and mouse-eaten libraries, that were designed and collected by men who voted with Grattan are perhaps as mournful in the end as the four mudwalls that are so often left in Wicklow as the only remnants of a farmhouse.
(*Essay: 'A Landlord's Garden in County Wicklow'*)

The Irish theatre

It is vital to note that apart from some evidence of early liturgical drama, there is little drama of importance and no original Irish theatre until the late nineteenth century. After the Restoration of Charles II to the English throne in 1660, John Ogilby, a Scottish Master of the Revels, had built the first professional theatre in Ireland — the Smock Alley Theatre in Dublin — but this became the preserve of the resident ruling class who took their standards and their plays from London. Consequently, Dublin acted as host to a stream of visiting productions headed by leading actors such as David Garrick (1717—79). At the same time , Smock Alley Theatre became a breeding ground for Irish talent both in acting and playwriting. The problem was that this did little to improve the state of the Irish theatre since outstanding players such as Peg Woffington (c. 1714—60) and Charles Macklin (c. 1700—97), not to mention a line of influential playwrights from George Farquhar (1678—1707) to Oscar Wilde (1854—1900), chose to abandon their native country for the greater opportunities offered by the London theatre scene. Thus the Irish had a great effect on the development of the English stage whilst Ireland herself was denied a native tradition.

The Irish stage in the second half of the nineteenth century was dominated by the staple fare of the English touring company, the 'popular' drama typified by Melodrama, in which the plots are contrived and conventional and caricature takes the place of character. Some Irish playwrights, most notably Dion Boucicault (1822—90), author of *The Colleen Bawn* and over a hundred other plays, successfully exploited a commercial brand of 'Irishness', but others, particularly during the 1880's, strove for a genuine Irish theatre which fought against the tradition personified by, amongst other things, the 'stage Irishman', — 'that scarecrow' as Yeats called him. This caricature of the typical Irishman presented him as indolent and harmlessly garrulous when he was not drunken and violent, speaking a peculiar artificial language, full of expressions rarely if ever used by real Irish peasants, such as 'Begorrah'and 'Bejabbers'. There was a real danger that Irish theatregoers might even accept this debased image of themselves unless some authentic alternative were created out of the anger felt by the new breed of dramatists at this travesty.

During the nineteenth century, the growing tide of Irish Nationalism began to penetrate literary circles just as it was affecting every other aspect of life. In 1892, the year after he had founded the Irish Literary Society in London, W.B. Yeats founded the *National Literary Society* in Dublin, to be followed in 1893 by Douglas Hyde and others who formed the *Gaelic League*. Whereas Yeats was Anglo-Irish, speaking little or no Gaelic, the Gaelic League wished to encourage a new literature written in Irish, seeking a revival of many cultural traditions. This aim was shared by Yeats but the Gaelic League was far more 'narrow' in its political affiliations, seeing literary and theatrical activity as an intrinsic part of the growing movement towards Home Rule and the 'de-Anglicization' of Ireland. It was this narrowness of vision which always separated Hyde and his followers from Yeats and his supporters, a division which was barely noticeable at first but which became more and more pronounced after the turn of the century as political activity became more intense. Synge's membership of the *Irish League,* which was founded by Maud Gonne to provide an opportunity for Irish nationalists in France to co-ordinate their efforts to help achieve Irish independence, lasted only three months. His attitude towards Nationalism is revealed in his letter of resignation where he states that he could never ally himself with what he described as 'a revolutionary and semi-military movement.' (Letter to Maud Gonne, quoted in Greene and Stephens, *J.M. Synge 1871–1909*).

Between 1892 and 1899 Yeats discussed with other interested parties the possibility of opening a small theatre in Dublin in the hope of showing

> that Ireland is not the home of buffoonery and of sentiment, as it has been represented, but the home of an ancient idealism.
> *(Prospectus of the Irish Literary Theatre)*

As a result, the *Irish Literary Theatre* was launched in May 1899 with a double-bill of Yeats's *The Countess Cathleen* and *The Heather Field* by Edward Martyn, a Mayo landowner greatly interested in the theatre. George Moore, the novelist and critic, and the widowed Lady Augusta Gregory, who was the most practically minded of the four, were the other founder members. Subsequently various plays were performed in hired halls employing professional English actors but in 1901 Yeats brought about a merger with a company of amateur Irish actors run by the brothers William and Frank Fay, the union giving rise to the *Irish National Theatre Society*.

The nomadic nature of that organisation came to an end with the intervention of Miss Annie Horniman, the wealthy daughter of a Manchester industrialist, whose interest in the theatre was fired by the Society's presentation of several plays at a hall in Kensington during a London tour in 1904. It was Miss Horniman's money which paid for the conversion in Dublin of what had been the Mechanics' Institute and neighbouring mortuary into the now world-famous *Abbey Theatre*. Thus Yeats's 'wing' of the Irish Theatre Movement had found a home and financial backing.

The policy of the company and its leaders may be summed up in Lady Gregory's words: 'We went on giving what we thought good until it became popular.' Plays were written or chosen to fulfil Yeats's desire to show Ireland as 'the home of an ancient idealism', often drawing upon Gaelic legend and history made available in translation from Old and Middle Irish by scholars such as Douglas Hyde. Allied to explorations of mythical material were comedies and plays by Lady Gregory herself and writers, such as Edward Martyn, who drew their inspiration and language from traditional forms of peasant and rural life.

The artistic style of this company, which attracted Synge, was revolutionary. In order to ensure that the play itself was the focus of attention, the emphasis was on beauty and simplicity in all aspects of stage presentation. Sets were as simple as possible, consisting usually of dyed curtains and screens, plain wooden furniture and properties made of papier-mâché. Costumes were simple and often hand-dyed in symbolic colours. In performing Yeats's verse plays in particular, the actors were directed in such a way as to rule out any unnecessary stage movement and were trained to speak the verse in such a way as to bring out its poetic beauty. All of this was in deliberate contrast to the commercial English stage at the time with its elaborate sets and costumes and dominated by its 'Star System'. William Fay, the manager of the Abbey Company, worked towards a 'natural' approach more appropriate to the more realistic plays in the repertoire and in contrast to the 'symbolic' approach of Yeats. The combination of these two methods of production peculiarly suited the company in its presentation of Synge's brand of poetic realism.

Synge at the Abbey Theatre

From 1896, when he first met Yeats in Paris, Synge obviously knew of the literary and theatrical developments taking place in Dublin and yet he long remained apart from them. It was not until 1903, with the Abbey's production of *In the Shadow of the Glen*, that he became actively involved with the company itself. From the outset Synge's plays became a subject of critical controversy. His presentation of the character of Nora was seen as a slur on Irish womanhood and, although *Riders to the Sea* proved a minor success with the Dublin critics in that at least it was not attacked, *The Well of the Saints*, produced in 1905, was berated for its 'un-Irishness'. Beginning to realise the extent of the Irish critics' 'sensitivity' to his view of Irish life, Synge withheld *The Tinker's Wedding* from publication, and the Abbey Theatre did not perform this comedy about the life of vagrants, anticipating the reception it could expect on the grounds of its anti-clericalism.

Therefore, by the time of the production of *Playboy* in 1907, it can have come as no surprise to Synge, or to the rest of the directors and company, especially in view of the rumours that had been circulated that the play was 'in praise of murder', that uproar should have been the result. The actors put great pressure on Synge to change and cut lines but to little avail. Willie Fay wrote:

> We might as well have tried to move the Hill of Howth as move Synge. That was his play, he said, and, barring one or two jots and tittles of 'bad language' that he grudgingly consented to excise, it was the play that with a great screwing up of courage we produced. (*The Fays of the Abbey Theatre*)

Lady Gregory's requests for cuts were similarly ignored although Synge did sacrifice Pegeen's lines about the Widow Quin nursing a black ram at her breast and Michael James's description of the men retching at the wake. Prompted by Lady Gregory, sensible of the reactions aroused previously by his use of language, Synge also wrote a programme note intended to deflect criticism but which was, in effect, interpreted as a challenge and only served to fuel his critics' wrath.

After apparently receiving the first act well, the audience became increasingly puzzled during Act 2 and at Christy's line (p. 106), mistakenly altered by Willie Fay to 'a drift of Mayo girls standing in their shifts itself', the theatre resounded with boos and cat-calls. The word 'drift' would normally only be used of cattle, and 'shift' (quite apart from the indecent picture of Irish girls in their underwear) was directly associated with Kitty O'Shea, Parnell's mistress. According to Padraic Colum, the audience's response had noticeably stiffened from the moment of Old Mahon's entry. His appearance was extremely realistic and had the effect of introducing an essentially non-comic element into the play. The review in *The Freeman's Journal* which inveighed against 'this unmitigated, protracted libel upon Irish peasant men and, worse still, upon Irish peasant girlhood' sounded the note so often encountered in the many articles on the play which filled the Dublin press. Synge was dubbed 'the dramatist of the dung heap' by *The Evening Mail* for, in seeking to reject the image of the 'stage Irishman', he had offended against the new image of the Catholic peasant as the repository of noble qualities. Between these two extremes there was no room for Synge's more realistic approach.

It was Yeats, recalled from Scotland by Lady Gregory's telegram, who took up the battle on behalf of *Playboy*. The directors determined that, in Yeats's words, 'We will go on until the play has been heard sufficiently to be judged on its merits'. The police were called in in an attempt to ensure that the actors would get a hearing and Yeats employed a claque of students in support. Throughout the week there were many arrests followed by court hearings and fines. Fights broke out both in and around the theatre. *Playboy* was firmly established as a *cause célèbre* and further similar disturbances were to follow its production in America.

Interviewed on the second night of the play, when he was described by the reporter as 'excited and restless', Synge, who had wisely stayed aloof from previous controversies over his plays, announced that he 'wrote the play because it pleased me' and he didn't 'care a rap how the people take it'. His tactlessness, quite typical of his attitude towards his work, although at variance with his diplomatic behaviour at other times, hardly cooled the situation.

Yeats called a public debate at the theatre the following week, which Synge's ill-health prevented him from attending, but the poet bravely addressed a packed auditorium which was almost totally hostile. According to Lady Gregory's account, the audience was finally forced to listen to Yeats's lecture on the freedom of the theatre which enlarged upon the view he had shouted above the mayhem of the previous week:

> Every man has a right to hear it and condemn it if he pleases but no man has a right to interfere with another man hearing a play and judging for himself. The country that condescends either to bully or to permit to be bullied soon ceases to have any fine qualities.

Synge, whom Yeats was to describe as being 'so absorbed in his own vision of the world that he cares for nothing else', was indeed fortunate in having such a champion.

Commentary

What is the play about?

On the surface, *Playboy* is concerned to present us with a particular
view of the Irish peasantry at the turn of the century, demonstrating
the problems confronting a rural community whose most vigorous
offspring have emigrated, leaving behind such evils as physical
deprivation and arranged marriages. Life in this isolated community
set in the Congested Districts is clearly harsh and poverty-stricken
— far removed from the relatively privileged life-style of Synge's
own family. The violence and cruelty of the characters, although
humorously presented, is constantly emphasised, balancing the
warmth and energy which can be equally observed in their conduct
and speech. The reality of Synge's creation is such that the audience
is made aware of the potential both for good and bad that is present
in each one of the characters. Here is no romantic view of a
deprived peasant class but a satirical presentation of an enclosed
community which possesses only in embryo the imaginative charm
and power traditionally associated with the Irish.

Synge demonstrates the ability of this community to create a
hero in its own likeness as a form of wish fulfilment. The story of
the boy who says he killed his father is used to reveal the true
nature of these characters who represent a class held in thrall by the
paternal authority of the Catholic Church. It was the treatment of
religious attitudes — for example, Christy's statement that he
killed his father with the help of God (p. 51) and Shawn's
exaggerated deference to Father Reilly and the Church — which
fuelled the furore surrounding the play. Synge's deliberately comic
presentation of this aspect of peasant life provoked a not surprising
hostility in many of his contemporaries.

This satirical treatment of his subject matter, however, allows
Synge to move into the realms of more abstract exploration of the
themes involved in the plot. Throughout the play there is a fine
balance maintained between the *reality* of what happens and the
poetry inherent in the characters, particularly Christy and Pegeen.
They share a fear of the dark and 'lonesomeness', a need to find

and establish their own real identities. In their lovemaking, it is as if their true natures become apparent to them for the first time. The situation in which they are trapped forces Pegeen to renounce Christy but, by contrast, he grows in stature through a series of rebuffs, to the point where he can in effect 'kill' the power of his father, if not the man himself. Thus he can leave Pegeen grieving while he is secure in his new identity as a 'young gaffer'.

Through Christy's development, the audience is led on an exploration of the romance of illusion. At his first entry, the villagers, deprived of colour and excitement, seize upon the mystery of the stranger and, thus encouraged, his story grows from 'I just riz the loy and let fall the edge of it on the ridge of his skull' (p. 52) to a catalogue of deeds of derring-do. The villagers believe him because they *need* the excitement, the feeling of importance that comes from knowing a celebrity; Synge enjoys the irony that they gain this excitement from someone of Christy's slight stature. In careful contrast to the great mythical heroes who figure in Yeats's plays, Christy is a Don Quixote, a figure of fun, never a serious contender for the role of hero. The power of illusion is such that to the villagers and to himself he can nevertheless be a hero, at least until the illusion is shattered by the intrusion of reality in the person of Old Mahon.

It is possible to see in *Playboy* many literary and mythical echoes and parallels. In his contribution to what may be termed the Literature of the Grotesque, Synge would seem to be portraying the image of society as if reflected in Christy's distorting mirror. In this world 'a fine madness' seems to dominate at one level and yet it is peopled by essentially crippled characters whose mental abilities have been thwarted and stunted by their physical and imaginative environment. It is significant that in her definition of 'this place', Pegeen lists as the inhabitants 'red Linahan, has a squint in his eye, and Patcheen is lame in his heel, or the mad Mulrannies were driven from California and they lost their wits.' (p. 43)

The two most commonly drawn parallels are with the myths of Christ and Oedipus. The analogy with the story of Christ has been taken to extremes, for instance: 'It is through his exploitation in *Playboy* of the ministry and crucifixion of Jesus that Synge crystallized the elements of the play into a coherent masterpiece.' (Article by Sultan in Maurice Harmon (ed.): *The Celtic Master*) Certainly the Epiphany, when the three Magi brought gifts to the infant Jesus, would seem to be parodied in the bringing of presents

by the Village Girls; and echoes of the entry into Jerusalem can be
seen in Christy's triumphant entry into the house after his victory
ride on a donkey to be followed by a judgment scene in which the
crowd's mood changes. The binding and wounding of Christy
recalls that of Christ just as his projected hanging echoes the
crucifixion. And Pegeen's betrayal is Judas-like. As Robin Skelton
points out:

> If we see Christy Mahon as a distorted reflection of Christ
> Messiah, then we can see Father Reilly and the Holy Father
> and Shawn Keogh as representatives of the Old Testament
> religion and those Saducees and Pharisees whom Christ opposed.'
> (*The Writings of J.M. Synge*)

That this parallel is intended by Synge must surely be proved not
least by Old Mahon's rhetorical question to his son '. . . isn't it by
the like of you the sins of the whole world are committed?' (p. 103),
reminding us quite deliberately of Christ who took upon Him all
the sins of the world. It must nevertheless be remembered that the
analogy is intermittent; it cannot be traced slavishly in every aspect
of the play but is one layer among many.

Similarly with Oedipus, who, according to Greek mythology,
killed his father and married his mother: Christy is after all, by his
own admission, guilty of killing his 'da', representing, according to
the words of the reviewer in the Dublin *Evening Mail* after the first
performance 'some kind of nation-killer whom Irish men and Irish
women hasten to lionize'; and it was the hope of Old Mahon to
marry his son to the widow who had nursed him. The parallels
are obvious but again Synge's intention is more akin to parody
rather than straightforward analogy. Where the position of Oedipus
is archetypally tragic, Christy's crime, for all its serious undertones,
is presented as the subject of comedy, and does not in the end take
place anyway.

Thus the thematic content of *Playboy* should be understood as
being of a piece with the style of the play. What seems at first
glance a humorous satire on Irish peasant life centres upon those
universal qualities and preoccupations which are the subject of
myth.

What kind of play is it?

'A comedy, an extravaganza, made to amuse' was Synge's definition
of *Playboy* given to an *Evening Mail* reporter after the first night
riots. In a letter to the *Irish Times*, however, he wrote:

The Playboy is not a play with a 'purpose' in the modern sense
of the word but although parts of it are or are meant to be
extravagant comedy, still a great deal that is in it and a great
deal more that is behind it is perfectly serious when looked at in
a certain light.

Given that Synge himself points us simultaneously in different
directions with regard to the true nature and purpose of his play,
the question of which genre of dramatic writing *Playboy* should be
consigned to is, not surprisingly, a complex one. How far is it
'merely' a comedy 'made to amuse', and how far 'perfectly serious'?
What effect does the serious element have upon the quality of the
comedy? To answer such questions it is necessary to look at Synge's
knowledge and use of, and attitude towards, other literary sources
in the development of his own dramatic style.

As Maurice Bourgeois has pointed out at length in *John
Millington Synge and the Irish Theatre*, Synge was certainly well
acquainted with the work of a majority of French novelists and
prose-writers. Balzac, Flaubert, Maupassant, Zola and Huysmans all
featured strongly in his studies but, as can be seen from Synge's
rejection of Zola in the Preface to *Playboy*, to read an author is not
necessarily to be in agreement with his aims and methods, still less
to be influenced by him to the extent of being called derivative, let
alone a plagiarist. Synge's knowledge of developments in dramatic
technique from early farce through to Ibsen was extensive; it is
indeed apparent from the eleven extant drafts of *Playboy* that he
worked on plot and character development in terms of techniques
he himself labelled, for example, as 'Molièrean' or 'Rabelaisian'. His
working methods reveal that Synge was consciously using models
of past writers as a means of developing his own dramatic writing.

In terms of the Unities of Time, Place and Action which Aristotle
observed in Greek tragedy, *Playboy* is constructed according to
'the rules'. The entire action of the play takes place within twenty
four hours between one autumn evening and the next; the setting is
the single location of Michael James Flaherty's shebeen and the
entire plot concerns the appearance, experience and final ousting
of the Playboy. Synge also borrows the classical device of the
Chorus in the use of the crowd to comment upon the action of the
main characters in the last 'scene' of Act Three and, most noticeably,
in his presentation of the race which leads to Christy's crowning.
The reporting of an exciting crucial event, rather than its enactment,
is carefully devised and highly successful. These aspects of the

structure of the play Synge arrived at gradually through a long process of revision and re-writing. His original scenario began with the actual 'murder' of Old Mahon in a potato field but gradually this was changed to the reporting of the crime by Christy, which allows a subtle development of 'the power of the lie'. Some changes were made by Synge to facilitate the staging of the play and to accommodate it to the resources of the Abbey Theatre, but it is important to realise how closely the basic technique of the play underpins its subject matter. It is more than a happy coincidence that a mock-heroic extravagant comedy employs devices developed for the presentation of full-blown mythical drama as in the Classical Theatre of Ancient Greece.

Conventional features of comedy do abound in *Playboy* as, for example, in the contrasting appearance and attitudes of the 'comic couple' of Jimmy and Philly, the verbal humour of the exchanges between Pegeen and the Widow when they compete for Christy, and the visual, often violent, comic effects such as Christy's biting Shawn's leg. Quite apart from anything else, the play abounds in jokes and witty repartee. And yet there is so much more to the play than would be suggested by the straightforward description 'comedy'.

In the search to identify the essential qualities that mark *Playboy* as a comic creation owing a significant debt to established writers and dramatic techniques, the Preface proves a most helpful document. In condemning the plays of Ibsen and Zola for 'dealing with the reality of life in joyless and pallid works' (p. 40) and stressing his own desire for a stage that presented both 'reality' and 'joy', Synge is pointing towards the source of his unique qualities as a dramatist. Rejecting the dominant mode of European drama of the early twentieth century with its concentration on what Thomas Kilroy has termed 'the articulate life of the bourgeoisie', Synge's own brand of 'realism', through the depiction of Irish peasant life, strove to re-instate a delight in life in *all* its aspects. Synge's attitude towards his subject matter is clarified in a letter about *Playboy* to M.J. Nolan on 19 February 1907 — the play shows, he says, that 'the wildness and, if you will, vices of the Irish peasantry are due, like their extraordinary good points of all kinds, to the *richness* of their nature — a thing that is priceless beyond words.'

In answering critics who, far from seeing *Playboy* as in any way realistic sought to condemn the subject matter as being totally fantastic, Synge cited two well-documented cases of murderers who had been sheltered by the local population to prevent their arrest by the police. As he made clear in a letter to Stephen Mackenna, however, Synge only used this as a defence because he was attacked — 'I used the cases afterwards to controvert critics who said it was impossible'. Indeed the idea for the play was undoubtedly sown by a story he heard on his travels in the Aran Islands, but the crucial difference introduced by Synge is the tone of the telling of the tale. The islander who told him about the man concealed from the police spoke with tremendous seriousness of protecting a man who had already suffered enough in being driven to commit the worst crime known to man, but this is *not* the tone of *Playboy*. Synge uses his material to create a satirical comedy of peasant life, the ironic tone of which enables him to provide a tragic undertow to the whole piece which culminates in Pegeen's grief-striken outburst at the end of the play.

Thus the tone of the play is the key to the mock-heroic parody. Christy, like Don Quixote to whom Synge made reference in talking about the play, is essentially a mock-heroic creation. He is presented as a cowardly young layabout who yet grows in stature sufficient to be able to win the games but this very development is itself undercut by the reappearance of Old Mahon. Even when Christy apparently triumphs and leaves to lead a life of 'romancing' the audience, whilst treasuring his lively imagination, cannot fail to realise that his 'herosim' is hardly on a par with the heroes of the myths. In Synge's picture of contemporary peasant life, this is the level to which heroes are reduced; there is no room for a new Cuchulain.

It should by now be apparent that Synge is essentially an eclectic writer. Both in his use and creation of language and in his dramatic method, he takes from a wide variety of sources only what he needs and then creates from this diversity a unique entity. His approach to the presentation of Irish life on the stage demonstrates both his integrity as an artist and prefigures the preoccupations later seen in the work of dramatists like Samuel Beckett. Born in the nineteenth century Synge is essentially a twentieth-century writer whose attitudes and insights, although presented humorously, are serious, even tragic, in their implications.

Notes on the characters

Christy Mahon
Christy's first appearance is hardly what is expected from the word 'Playboy'. He is 'a slight young man . . . very tired and frightened

and dirty' (p.48) who confesses to being 'slow at learning' (p.49).
His shyness is obvious and in his own words, to Pegeen's
disappointment, he is 'a quiet, simple fellow with no man giving me
heed' (p.57). Basking in the light of new-found admiration,
particularly the interest of Pegeen, he is encouraged to acquire a
greater degree of self-confidence, demonstrating a power to
describe through hyperbolic exaggeration, for example, when he
speaks of Old Mahon 'shying clods against the visage of the stars'
(p.58), but the tenuous nature of this new self-confidence is
immediately emphasised by his 'clinging to Pegeen' (p.59) at the
sound of a knock on the door. Gradually Christy's intense desire
for self-importance begins to be gratified as he listens to Pegeen
and the Widow competing for him. His naiveté is touchingly
established at the close of Act One in his delight at his new
situation.

Although Old Mahon's description of Christy is obviously
exaggerated, the exaggeration shares those very qualities evident in
Christy's description of his father. Synge's presentation of father
and son so as to exploit their similarities and differences is a vital
element in the success of the comedy. There is enough of 'the young
streeler' in Christy to support Old Mahon's view of him, and yet
the father's dismissal of his son's interest in nature (p.81) underlines
that quality in Christy which Synge always saw as admirable in
mankind. Old Mahon's desire to be the centre of attention finds its
counterpart and logical extension in Christy's development from
'a talker of folly' (p.80) into 'a likely gaffer' (p.110).

From hesitant beginnings, Christy builds an image of himself
both through the eyes of the villagers and through his own
imagination by means of the 'power of the lie', punningly based by
Synge upon the 'power of the loy'. Each time he tells his story,
Christy adds details which dramatically increase the nature of his
prowess. Acting up to the image expected of him he paints verbal
pictures of 'heroic' deeds which entrance his hearers, turn the local
girls into his worshippers and bring him Pegeen's love — even
though she tells him sharply that she has heard 'that story six times
since the dawn of day' (p.71).

Synge draws attention to Christy's vanity, in which he is so like
his father, in the opening soliloquy to Act Two. At this point
Christy's vision of future happiness is essentially limited: 'Well,
this'd be a fine place to be my whole life talking out with swearing
Christians . . . and I stalking around, smoking my pipe and drinking
my fill' (p.64).

However, his ambitions grow as he acquires the self-confidence
to pursue those dreams of freedom which only he and Pegeen are
capable of dreaming. Through his love for Pegeen — bolstered by
her passionate intensity, which leads him to feel a blasphemous
'kind of pity for the Lord God is all ages sitting lonesome in His
golden chair' (p.95) — it becomes possible for him to resemble in
reality the hero of their mutual dreams. The romantic imagination
he shows increasingly in his private conversations with Pegeen leads
the audience to accept his final assertion that he will 'go romancing
through a romping lifetime from this hour to the dawning of the
Judgment Day' (p.110), that he has indeed become 'The Playboy
of the Western World'. Transformed into the brave fellow he is
mistaken for, Christy's belief in himself — 'I'm mounted on the
spring tide of the stars of luck, the way it'll be good for any to
have me in the house' (p.101) — survives the fickleness of the
crowd and the treachery of Pegeen. And yet this Playboy is hardly
on a par with heroes like Cuchulain. He has, for instance, a
distinctive — rather unheroic — way of spitting; and even when
winning the race, he only narrowly avoids getting stuck in a bog,
whilst the donkey he is riding is described as 'kicking the stars'
(p.91). Through such contrasts Synge would seem to be emphasising
that for a community whose attitudes and aspirations lead it to
revere, for example, Daneen Sullivan who 'knocked the eye from a
peeler' (p.43), the likes of Christy Mahon are appropriate
contemporary heroes rather than the *truly* heroic figures from
Ireland's mythical past.

Pegeen Mike

Synge's presentation of female characters had caused uproar from
1903 onwards when the portrait of Nora in *In the Shadow of the
Glen* was 'felt to be a slur on Irish womanhood' (T.R. Henn:
Introduction to *The Complete Plays*). Pegeen Mike is hardly the
'respectable and likeable country girl' that William Fay begged
Synge to create (Kilroy: *The 'Playboy' Riots*).

'A wild-looking but fine girl of about twenty' (p.41), Pegeen in
her opening speech reveals a desire for the finery of respectability
(including the 'fine-tooth comb' so often equated with romantic
ladies in traditional ballads) as well as her lack of education in the
slowness with which she writes. Through her treatment of Shawn
in their first conversation, her scorn and impatience with his
sycophantic, cowardly nature help to establish her own independent
cast of mind. She is hardly a girl to stand in fear of paternal

authority whether it be represented by the Church or her own father. Jimmy's description of her as 'a fine girl would knock the heads of any two men in the place' seems accurate, underlining her difference from the traditional gentle 'feminine' heroines.

A victim of the convention of the arranged marriage, Pegeen is demonstrably being given to an unsuitable husband in her weak cousin Shawn, despite his assertion to the contrary, for there is no way in which Shawn could appreciate the strength of the desire for freedom and excitement which is the core of Pegeen's emotional life. Trapped by her dull existence, Pegeen seizes upon the 'heroic' aspects of Christy's deed as an example of the adventurous vitality she instinctively knows that life should possess. Attracted to Christy, she takes up the words of the 'soft lad' (p.51) and transforms him through her imaginative vitality into the Playboy of the Western World. Previously her amazing facility with words has been largely directed at quelling others, for instance, the Village Girls and, by her own admission, turning her into 'the fright of seven townlands for my biting tongue' (p.97). But now, under the influence of Christy's love and admiration, she becomes capable of speaking in tones of 'real tenderness' (p.96).

It is Pegeen's very intensity of feeling, however, that also lies at the root of her betrayal of Christy. The brutal savagery that is an intrinsic part both of the world she lives in and of her own nature, is revealed most clearly in her burning of Christy's leg; but this is consistent with her violent jealousy and the verbal torture she inflicts on Christy by describing a hanging in graphic detail (p.72). She 'persuades' Christy to confess his deed by threatening him with a broom and sees Shawn off with a box on the ear at the end of the play. Physical violence is merely one manifestation of Pegeen's frustrated energy, an energy which hungers for the romance of independence and yet brings that pride and integrity which leads her to reject Christy. He has fooled her and therefore she turns her back on her chance of a life away from the sordid reality she has always known. It is only as Christy leaves that she realises just what she has lost; she is raised above the likes of her father simply because she is capable of apprehending her loss. She alone could have responded to the wider horizons offered by the life of the imagination. In love with the romantic *idea* of heroic parricide, when apparently confronted with the deed itself, Pegeen demonstrates a mean-spirited hypocrisy. Her character epitomises the clash between dream and reality in the Irish mentality which Synge is subtly exposing.

Widow Quin

In the isolated community of a village in the wilder part of County Mayo, Widow Quin suffers the treatment so often meted out to women in her position. Guilty of murdering her husband and having outlived her children, despite being only thirty years of age, she is an obvious candidate for the role of village 'witch'. Her notoriety attracts the Village Girls but Pegeen accuses her of 'rearing a black ram at your own breast' (p.62), implying that the Widow deals in black magic. Synge's presentation of this 'wicked' woman as the one person who ultimately does not desert Christy is a vital ingredient in the irony of the play.

When she first sees Christy, the Widow regards him with 'half-amused curiosity' (p.60), seeing her fellow murderer as more suited 'to saying your catechism than slaying your da' (p.60). Keen to establish 'kinship' with Christy, she emphasises her greater fitness for his company than the young flirtatious Pegeen, pulling Christy to his feet in her attempt to, as she says, carry out the word of Shawn and Father Reilly by taking him off to her cottage. Despite Pegeen's taunts, the Widow retains her essential good humour throughout her lively verbal competition for possession of Christy. When Christy timidly chooses Pegeen, the Widow takes her defeat well, but cannot resist a final shot at Pegeen's forthcoming marriage as she leaves (p.62).

It is the Widow who enters Christy for the sports and her pleasure at Susan nominating him 'to make a second husband to the Widow Quin' (p.70) is evident. Where the Young Girls are instantly intimidated by Pegeen Mike's anger, the Widow's reaction is more insolent. She has the self-confidence of a mature independence necessitated by her position in this enclosed society.

Always willing to scheme and connive, the Widow, having demanded Shawn's 'red cow' and 'mountainy ram', 'the right of way across your rye path and a load of dung at Michaelmas and turbary upon the western hill' (p.78), happily joins Shawn's plan to be rid of Christy. Moreover, Synge reinforces this aspect of the Widow's character when she is shown setting up a similar bargain with Christy; it would seem that she will plot wherever necessary to further her own material welfare. However, this view of the Widow must be qualified by her continuing support for Christy in the face of the fickle crowd. Although she seems more aware of Christy's true nature than any other character, it is she who tries to effect his escape, albeit in the ludicrous disguise of Sara's petticoat; despite her impatience with his continuing desire to remain with Pegeen, she is reluctant to see Christy 'stifled on the gallows tree' (p.106).

Throughout, the Widow maintains her distance from the action. She is hardly surprised by the entry of the supposedly dead Old Mahon but remains supportive to Christy:

> I with my little houseen above where there'd be myself to tend you, and none to ask were you a murderer or what at all. (p.84)

Even when her offer of help, and presumably marriage, is rejected, she does not desert him but reverts to her attitude of amused observer, the traditional stance of an outsider:

> Well, if the worst comes in the end of all, it'll be great game to see there's none to pity him but a widow woman, the like of me, has buried her children and destroyed her man.

Synge's own interest in this particular character is obvious from the development of the play through the various drafts from 1904—7. As Robin Skelton points out 'The Widow Quin several times appears about to dominate the play and her part has to be adjusted to the demands of the whole' (*The Writings of J.M. Synge*). Thus by a constant process of revision, we are given the final creation of a woman who on the surface is undesirable and full of machinations, yet, ironically, is the only person possessing true charity and kindness. Significantly, unlike such as Shawn, the Widow is given only two references to God in the entire play. In her mixture of detached amusement, sympathy and opportunism, she, more than any other character, is capable of perceiving the reality of the situation and the true nature of the protagonists.

Old Mahon

According to his son, Old Mahon is a crude, boorish, lazy man, given to great bouts of drinking, swearing and fighting. To bolster his own self-image, Christy also describes his father as a 'strong' farmer (p.49) i.e. a man of substance, and yet insists that his father was determined to marry him to the 45 year-old, blind and lame Widow Casey so that he would gain possession of 'her hut to live in and her gold to drink' (p.68).

When the old man, who, far from being a prosperous farmer, is nothing more than a squatter, finally appears, he plainly has been frequently drunk (pp.92—3). He rants and raves, alternating between threats of revenge and bouts of self-pity, but hardly lives up to the deliberately exaggerated picture drawn by Christy. Old

Mahon is a bully who seeks to terrorize his son but at the same time is proud of his bandaged head since it brings him the attention he craves just as being placed in a straitjacket in an asylum is a matter for boasting since it was an occasion when 'seven doctors' wrote out his 'sayings in a printed book' (p.93). When Christy finally refuses to bow down to his father's will, insisting that from now on it will be Old Mahon who will be 'stewing my oatmeal and washing my spuds' (p.110), Old Mahon is delighted to find such a capacity for domineering in the son he had considered nothing but 'an ugly young streeler with a murderous gob' (p.79). His vanity will be well satisfied by the life of 'romancing' envisaged by Christy.

Shawn Keogh

During his attempt to bribe Christy to leave Pegeen, Shawn describes himself as 'a quiet, simple fellow' who 'wouldn't raise a hand upon her if she scratched itself' (p.77). From his first entry, when he apparently betrays such terror of the disapproval of the parish priest that he is not prepared to keep his fiancée company during the long, dark night, Shawn's timid nature and fear of authority, particularly that represented by the Catholic Church, is obvious, demonstrating a sham piety that is nothing more than a façade for Shawn's innate cowardice. He hides his real fear of being in the isolated pub after dark behind a socially acceptable deference to the Church. Pegeen's dismissal of him as a 'middling kind of scarecrow' (p.99) and her father's assessment that such as Shawn could only father 'puny weeds' (p.102) seem more than justified.

Throughout, Shawn is the butt of the other men's humour which is often cruel, as in Act One when they try to force him to stay to keep Pegeen company (p.45−7). But such is the ludicrous nature of Shawn's cringing attitude and over-religiosity, there is never any likelihood of the audience sympathising with him. Since he is, however, the most overtly religious character with his constant appeals to God and various saints, as well as his obsession with the approval of Father Reilly, it is significant that in the last act, it is Shawn who encourages the men to torture Christy (p.108) and tells Pegeen to burn his leg with a lighted sod. Absolutely terrified that he might suffer physical hurt himself, he is determined to inflict as much suffering as possible upon his rival. There is no Christian compassion in this 'God-fearing' man, only a 'heathen' desire for revenge.

Michael James Flaherty

Owner of the shebeen, widower father of Pegeen, Michael James is essentially an adaptable man. From the beginning he is shown to be selfish and self-indulgent, more concerned to join in the drinking and merry-making at a nearby wake than to heed his daughter's complaints about being left alone. His rather sadistic teasing of Shawn hardly endears him to the audience although it is funny to watch. The dominant one of the three friends, he leads the questioning which prompts Christy to reveal the nature of his deed and, impressed by 'mister honey', delights in offering him sanctuary from the police, partly because it solves his immediate problem by providing him with a pot-boy who will keep Pegeen company. He sees no irony in his pleasure at leaving his daughter with a murderer.

Despite his obvious contempt for Shawn's cowardly nature, he is pleased to marry off his daughter to him, describing him as a 'decent Christian'; but when Pegeen insists upon her preference for Christy, Michael can again take this change of plan in his stride. His momentary objections to having a murderer for a son-in-law are soon allayed, and he ends up giving his father's blessing to the prospect of Pegeen and Christy's union.

Unhindered by any guiding principle, Michael seems able to make the best of any situation in which he finds himself. Although he frequently cites 'the will of God' in conversation, his Christianity is shown to be as superficial as the moralizing attitudes he finds it so easy to adopt, particularly when he is drunk. He professes to run a respectable tavern while at the same time selling illicit poteen. His ultimate desire is only to be left in peace to drink, a final attitude which emphasises Pegeen's total isolation in her wild lamentation for the loss of the Playboy.

Jimmy Farrell and Philly Cullen

As the jingle of their Christian names suggests, these two farmers are a 'comic couple', of the same age but of contrasting character, Philly being 'thin and mistrusting' and Jimmy, his physical and emotional opposite, being 'fat and amorous'. When Synge exploits these contrasts in their differing reactions, for example, to the Widow Quin's assertion that Old Mahon is insane (p.88), (Philly stating his disbelief while Jimmy is convinced she is telling the truth) he is using an age-old technique for creating individuality.

They are Michael James's drinking companions but their most important role within the play is to provide reactions to the words and actions of the central characters, particularly Christy. It is their function to provide 'local colour' as representative inhabitants of the area. They are central to the creation in Act One of the villagers' admiration of Christy's deed as well as establishing the cruelty apparently inherent to the area, whether this be shown humorously in their early teasing of Shawn or in a blacker vein in their final treatment of Christy. Their conversation about skulls at the opening of Act Two, based on a love of verbal exaggeration alongside a cheerful acceptance of the fact of death, lends credence to the Widow's description of the villagers' treatment of a local 'idiot', as well as preparing the audience for their later attitude to the Playboy.

With their obvious delight in drinking and festivities allied to those traits, Jimmy and Philly are convincingly created 'typical' Irishmen who in the cramping atmosphere of this drab, remote place retain a desire for colour and sensation which can only be appeased by drinking and crude escapades, such as the hanging of Jimmy's dog, and by endless exaggerated talk.

Village Girls

Created like the two farmers to provide a wider panorama against which the particular drama is enacted, the Village Girls are vitally important as foils for, and complementary to, the character of Pegeen Mike. Like her, they are easily impressed by any tale of 'heroic' endeavour but unlike Pegeen have no force of personality, hence their offering of pathetic excuses to explain away their presence in the face of Pegeen's anger (p.70). Their empty-headedness provides an excellent contrast to the scheming of the Widow Quin and yet the ease with which they, with the exception of Sara, turn against Christy forms a strong link with Pegeen's rejection of him. In their behaviour, Synge underlines the narrowness of vision of village life by demonstrating the foolishness of thoughtless hero-worship, a crucial aspect of his exploration of his theme, while their genuine enthusiasm shows the attraction of their own liveliness despite its mistaken object.

Synge's language

In the Preface to *Playboy*, Synge states that he has used 'one or two words only that I have not heard among the country people of Ireland or spoken in my own nursery before I could read the newspapers' and yet James Joyce asserted that Synge wrote 'a kind of fabricated language as unreal as his characters were unreal'. Where does the truth lie between these two apparently contradictory statements? How far does Synge reproduce peasant speech? To what should the range and liveliness of the language in *Playboy* be attributed?

It is first necessary to realise that in the dilemma confronting all Irish writers even today, Synge was at one with Yeats in seeing English as the appropriate language for the new Irish drama:

> With the present generation the linguistic atmosphere of Ireland has become definitely English enough, for the first time, to allow work to be done in English that is perfectly Irish in its essence, yet has sureness and purity of form. ('The Old and the New in Ireland', 1902.)

This attitude immediately won him enemies, particularly in Nationalist circles, but the English which Synge referred to here was not the English of the mainland. For a century and a half, after it was in effect re-introduced by the Cromwellian settlements of the 1650s, English remained isolated, the language of the land-owning class but cut off from mainstream English culture. Features of seventeenth-century English were preserved in Anglo-Irish long after they became obsolete in England. From the beginning of the nineteenth century onwards, the Irish-speaking population, encouraged by the relaxation of the Penal Laws and the resulting availability of education in the 'prestige' language of their rulers, began to acquire the English language — after all, to emigrate from the miseries of starvation usually meant going to America or England where Gaelic was of no value. The Anglo-Irish idiom consequently became, in Alan Price's words:

> . . . a form of English modified by Gaelic habits of speech, imagery and syntax. The words and meanings are those generally accepted wherever English is spoken but often the word-order corresponds to the word-order of Gaelic. (*Synge and Anglo-Irish Drama*)

In creating the poetic prose of *Playboy*, Synge took those elements of Anglo-Irish peasant speech, examples of which fill the many notebooks from his holidays in Aran, Kerry and Wicklow, using them as a basis for the language spoken by the characters. It is possible to cite many examples of his use of dialect forms, employing Gaelic syntax, such as the use of the present participle:

> It should be larceny, I'm thinking? (p.48);

the omission of relative pronouns and the use of the reflexive
pronoun:

> . . . a lad would kill his father, I'm thinking, would face . . .
> (p.53), . . . himself will stop along with you . . . (p.43);

and the use of the imperative:

> . . . and let you go off till you'd find a radiant lady . . . (p.100).

Obviously these and many other examples do bring a peculiarly
Irish flavour to the dialogue but it is not in this that the true
quality of Synge's language lies. It is demonstrably based on the
language of the peasants for the reasons already given but it would
certainly not have been possible at any time to find peasants
talking consistently in the manner of Synge's characters.
Consequently Synge's claims and Joyce's judgment are both
correct.

Examples can easily be found to substantiate Synge's claims for
authenticity in the realms of both language and plot. Conscious of
the attacks he could expect, the playwright's defence was to claim
that he was describing realistically the life of the Irish peasant. As
with the syntax, many examples can be found of how often he
delved into his notebooks for authentic peasant diction and ideas.
Pegeen Mike's accusation that the Widow Quin suckled a black ram
came from a story told to Synge by a Kerryman, Philly Harris, and
it was in Kerry too that he heard the grotesque tale of the
skeleton with 'thighs as long as your arm' (p.87). The Aran
notebooks are an even richer source of material. One from many
examples will indicate how Synge moulded his real-life observations
to create a dialogue which is rooted in a living language rather than
being merely a facsimile. In *The Aran Islands* Synge noted down
one of the islanders holding forth about being a bachelor:

> A man who is not married is no better than an old jackass. He
> goes into his sister's house, and into his brother's house; he eats
> a bit in this place, and a bit in another place, but he has no
> home for himself; like an old jackass straying on the rocks.

In his play Synge compresses and refines this speech:

> What's a single man, I ask you, eating a bit in one house and
> drinking a sup in another, like an old braying jackass strayed
> upon the rocks?

In terms of the language, *Playboy* excited opposition largely as a result of what D.J. O'Donoghue described in his letter to *The Freeman's Journal* as its 'continuous ferocity'. As the medium through which Synge expressed his ironic attitude toward the religiosity of many of his countrymen, the imagery of the play provoked indignant opposition. Whereas Synge saw the necessity that 'In a good play every speech should be as fully flavoured as a nut or an apple' and devised his poetic prose as a suitable vehicle, such phrases as Michael James's alliterative description of men at the wake 'stretched out retching speechless on the holy stones' (p.98) were seen as insulting to the nation. The heightened poetic nature of Christy's lovemaking to Pegeen was regarded as ludicrously inappropriate and, as in his reference to the 'lonesomeness' of God, on occasions blasphemous. It must often have seemed that Synge's critics were happier with the 'buffoon' image of the 'stage Irishman' and were incapable of appreciating Synge's intentions or achievement. In his uninhibited use of strong language Synge offended those Nationalists who, given the historical moment, could not accept any view of Ireland and the Irish which was anything other than one of shining purity.

A third attack with which Synge had to contend, was the suggestion first made in 1903 by Arthur Griffith, then editor of *The United Irishman,* that his writings were inspired not by matters truly Irish, but by 'the decadent cynicism that passes current in the Latin Quartier and the London salon'. While it is true that Synge's interest in things literary extended well beyond the shores of Ireland, as evidenced by his wide reading in several languages as well as the extensive periods of time he spent on the Continent, such an 'accusation' must be placed in true perspective. In the intentionally violent, rich and exaggerated imagery, many critics have drawn attention to the way Synge mirrors a linguistic debt to French writers, François Villon and Molière, the minor Elizabethan essayists and Marlowe. This is not, however, to suggest plagiarism, merely that Synge, like any other artist, was affected by what he read. Literature abounds in echoes and reflections of this nature. It may have seemed a sin to those devoted to the Nationalist cause but it is now accepted as demonstrating one way in which Synge's awareness of the potential of language was nourished.

An influence which those who were determined to attack him chose to ignore is the legacy of Gaelic poetry which had become far more accessible following the publication in 1893, in parallel texts, of the original Gaelic and Anglo-Irish translations of Douglas

Hyde's edition of *The Love Songs of Connacht*. Although the Anglo-Irish idiom had been used in a crude form by dramatists such as Dion Boucicault and novelists such as Samuel Lover and Charles Lever, Hyde managed for the first time to demonstrate its true possibilities which were taken up and explored more fully by Lady Gregory and Synge. Synge, in fact, took Hyde's book with him on his visits to Aran. All of his plays contain echoes of the songs of Connacht and the evidence of his notebooks shows that these were deliberately worked upon. That Synge's use of this language source was of a piece with his general method can be easily shown. In the song *Una Bhan* occurs the couplet:

> I had rather be beside her in a couch, ever kissing her,
> Than be sitting in heaven in the chair of the Trinity,

which contains the root of Christy's

> . . . and I squeezing kisses on your puckered lips till I'd feel a
> kind of pity for the Lord God is all ages sitting lonesome in his
> golden chair.

But Synge adapts his source material so as to include the sensuous image created by 'squeezing' and 'puckered' as well as building upon the recurring fear of 'lonesomeness' which runs throughout the play. A traditional image is extended to develop both Christy's character and the thematic content of the play.

Synge's approach to language is always consistent, his intentions always centring upon creating a dialogue to illustrate and explore all the potential of Anglo-Irish as part of a desire to restore the quality of 'joy' to the stage while endeavouring to remove 'squeamishness', a 'disease', which, he said in a letter to Stephen Mackenna, should be overcome because:

> Ireland will gain if Irish writers deal manfully, directly and
> decently with the entire reality of life.

Further reading

Synge's work

Robin Skelton (General Editor), *J.M. Synge: Collected Works*, Oxford University Press, 1961—8, 4 vols. Vols. III and IV (ed. Ann Saddlemyer) contain the plays along with manuscript and notebook material.

T.R. Henn (Editor), *The Complete Plays*, London: Eyre Methuen (Master Playwrights series), 1981. A shortened paperback version of T.R. Henn's edition of *The Plays and Poems of J.M. Synge*, London: Methuen, 1963.

M.Mac Liammoir (Editor), *Plays, Poems and Prose*, London: J.M. Dent (Everyman), 1961

Biography

David H. Greene and Edward M. Stephens, *J.M. Synge 1871—1907*, New York: Collier Macmillan, 1959. The only full biography of Synge

R. Skelton, *J.M. Synge and His World*, London: Thames and Hudson, 1971

Critical works

Alan Price, *Synge and Anglo-Irish Drama*, London: Methuen, 1961

Nicholas Grene, *Synge — A Critical Study of the Plays*, London: Macmillan, 1975

Ann Saddlemyer, *J.M. Synge and Modern Comedy*, Dublin: Dolmen Press, 1968

Robin Skelton, *The Writings of J.M. Synge*, London: Thames and Hudson, 1971

Declan Kiberd, *Synge and the Irish Language*, London: Macmillan, 1979

S.B. Bushrui (Editor), *A Centenary Tribute to John Millington Synge, 1871—1909: Sunshine and the Moon's Delight*, Gerrards Cross: Colin Smythe, 1979

Background books

J.C. Beckett, *The Making of Modern Ireland 1603—1923*, London, 1967

Una Ellis-Fermor, *The Irish Dramatic Movement*, London: Methuen, 1939; 2nd Edition, 1954

W.G. Fay and Catherine Carswell, *The Fays of the Abbey Theatre*, London: Rich and Cowan, 1935

Lady Augusta Gregory, *Our Irish Theatre. A Chapter of Autobiography*, New York: Putnam, 1939

Robert Kee, *The Green Flag*, London: Quartet Books, 1976. 3 vols., the second of which, *The Bold Fenian Men*, is the most directly relevant

V. Mercier, *The Irish Comic Tradition*, New York: O.U.P., 1962

Grenfell Morton, *Home Rule and the Irish Question*, London: Longman, 1980

W.B. Yeats, Various essays in *Explorations* and in *Essays and Introductions*, New York: Collier Books, 1968

Christy's first appearance in the shebeen (p. 34). National Theatre, 1976. (Photo: Haynes)

Christy with his new clothes in Act Two (*above*). Old Mahon and Pegeen in Act Three (*below*). National Theatre, 1976. (Photos: Haynes)

Pegeen and Christy in Act Three (*above*). The closing moments of the play: Christy 'on his knees face to face with Old Mahon', p. 109 (*below*). National Theatre, 1976. (Photos: Haynes)

The Playboy of the Western World

Persons in the play

CHRISTOPHER MAHON

OLD MAHON, his father, a squatter

MICHAEL JAMES FLAHERTY (called MICHAEL JAMES), a publican

MARGARET FLAHERTY (called PEGEEN MIKE), his daughter

WIDOW QUIN, a woman of about thirty

SHAWN KEOGH, her cousin, a young farmer

PHILLY CULLEN and JIMMY FARRELL, small farmers

SARA TANSEY, SUSAN BRADY and HONOR BLAKE, village girls

A BELLMAN

SOME PEASANTS

The action takes place near a village, on a wild coast of Mayo. The first Act passes on an evening of autumn, the other two Acts on the following day

Preface

In writing 'The Playboy of the Western World', as in my other plays, I have used one or two words only that I have not heard among the country people of Ireland, or spoken in my own nursery before I could read the newspapers. A certain number of the phrases I employ I have heard also from herds and fishermen along the coast from Kerry to Mayo or from beggar-women and ballad-singers nearer Dublin; and I am glad to acknowledge how much I owe to the folk-imagination of these fine people. Anyone who has lived in real intimacy with the Irish peasantry will know that the wildest sayings and ideas in this play are tame indeed, compared with the fancies one may hear in any little hillside cabin in Geesala, or Carraroe, or Dingle Bay. All art is a collaboration; and there is little doubt that in the happy ages of literature, striking and beautiful phrases were as ready to the story-teller's or the playwright's hand, as the rich cloaks and dresses of his time. It is probable that when the Elizabethan dramatist took his ink-horn and sat down to his work he used many phrases that he had just heard, as he sat at dinner, from his mother or his children. In Ireland, those of us who know the people have the same privilege. When I was writing *The Shadow of the Glen*, some years ago, I got more aid than any learning could have given me from a chink in the floor of the old Wicklow house where I was staying, that let me hear what was being said by the servant girls in the kitchen. This matter, I think, is of importance, for in countries where the imagination of the people, and the language they use, is rich and living, it is possible for a writer to be rich and copious in his words, and at the same time to give the reality, which is the root of all poetry, in a comprehensive and natural form. In the modern literature of towns, however, richness is found only in sonnets, or prose poems, or in one or two elaborate books that are far away from the profound and common interests of life. One has, on one side, Mallarmé and Huysmans producing this literature; and on the other, Ibsen and Zola dealing with the reality of life in joyless and pallid works. On the stage one must have reality, and one must have joy; and that is why the intellectual modern drama has failed, and people have grown sick of the false joy of the musical comedy, that has been given them in place of the rich joy found only in what is superb and wild in reality. In a good play every speech should be as fully flavoured as a nut or apple, and such speeches cannot be written by any one who works among people who have shut their lips on poetry. In Ireland, for a few years more, we have a popular imagination that is fiery, and magnificent, and tender; so that those of us who wish to write start with a chance that is not given to writers in places where the springtime of the local life has been forgotten, and the harvest is a memory only, and the straw has been turned into bricks.

J.M.S.

21st January, 1907.

The Playboy of the Western World

ACT I

*Country public house or shebeen, very rough and untidy.
There is a sort of counter on the right with shelves, holding many bottles and jugs, just seen above it. Empty barrels stand near the counter. At back, a little to left of
counter, there is a door into the open air, then, more to the
left, there is a settle with shelves above it, with more jugs,
and a table beneath a window. At the left there is a large
open fireplace, with turf fire, and a small door into inner
room. Pegeen, a wild-looking but fine girl, of about
twenty, is writing at table. She is dressed in the usual
peasant dress.*

PEGEEN [*Slowly as she writes*] Six yards of stuff for to
make a yellow gown. A pair of lace boots with lengthy
heels on them and brassy eyes. A hat is suited for a
wedding day. A fine-tooth comb. To be sent with
three barrels of porter in Jimmy Farrell's creel cart on
the evening of the coming Fair to Mister Michael James
Flaherty. With the best compliments of this season.
Margaret Flaherty.

SHAWN KEOGH [*A fat and fair young man comes in as she
signs, looks around awkwardly, when he sees she is
alone*] Where's himself?

PEGEEN [*Without looking at him*] He's coming. [*She directs letter*] To Mister Sheamus Mulroy, Wine and Spirit Dealer, Castlebar.

SHAWN [*Uneasily*] I didn't see him on the road.

PEGEEN How would you see him [*licks stamp and puts it on letter*] and it dark night this half-hour gone by?

SHAWN [*Turning towards door again*] I stood a while outside wondering would I have a right to pass on or to walk in and see you, Pegeen Mike [*comes to fire*], and I could hear the cows breathing and sighing in the stillness of the air, and not a step moving any place from this gate to the bridge.

PEGEEN [*Putting letter in envelope*] It's above at the crossroads he is, meeting Philly Cullen and a couple more are going along with him to Kate Cassidy's wake.

SHAWN [*Looking at her blankly*] And he's going that length in the dark night.

PEGEEN [*Impatiently*] He is surely, and leaving me lonesome on the scruff of the hill. [*She gets up and puts envelope on dresser, then winds clock*] Isn't it long the nights are now, Shawn Keogh, to be leaving a poor girl with her own self counting the hours to the dawn of day?

SHAWN [*With awkward humour*] If it is, when we're wedded in a short while you'll have no call to complain, for I've little will to be walking off to wakes or weddings in the darkness of the night.

PEGEEN [*With rather scornful good humour*] You're making mighty certain, Shaneen, that I'll wed you now.

SHAWN Aren't we after making a good bargain, the way we're only waiting these days on Father Reilly's dispensation from the bishops, or the Court of Rome.

PEGEEN [*Looking at him teasingly, washing up at dresser*]

It's a wonder, Shaneen, the Holy Father'd be taking notice of the likes of you; for if I was him I wouldn't bother with this place where you'll meet none but Red Linahan, has a squint in his eye, and Patcheen is lame in his heel, or the mad Mulrannies were driven from California and they lost in their wits. We're a queer lot these times to go troubling the Holy Father on his sacred seat.

SHAWN [*Scandalized*] If we are, we're as good this place as another, maybe, and as good these times as we were for ever.

PEGEEN [*With scorn*] As good it is? Where now will you meet the like of Daneen Sullivan knocked the eye from a peeler; or Marcus Quin, God rest him, got six months for maiming ewes, and he a great warrant to tell stories of holy Ireland till he'd have the old women shedding down tears about their feet. Where will you find the like of them, I'm saying?

SHAWN [*Timidly*] If you don't, it's a good job, maybe; for [*with peculiar emphasis on the words*] Father Reilly has small conceit to have that kind walking around and talking to the girls.

PEGEEN [*Impatiently throwing water from basin out of the door*] Stop tormenting me with Father Reilly [*imitating his voice*] when I'm asking only what way I'll pass these twelve hours of dark, and not take my death with the fear. [*Looking out of door*]

SHAWN [*Timidly*] Would I fetch you the Widow Quin, maybe?

PEGEEN Is it the like of that murderer? You'll not, surely.

SHAWN [*Going to her, soothingly*] Then I'm thinking himself will stop along with you when he sees you taking on; for it'll be a long night-time with great

darkness, and I'm after feeling a kind of fellow above
in the furzy ditch, groaning wicked like a maddening
dog, the way it's good cause you have, maybe, to be
fearing now.

PEGEEN [*Turning on him sharply*] What's that? Is it a
man you seen?

SHAWN [*Retreating*] I couldn't see him at all; but I heard
him groaning out, and breaking his heart. It should
have been a young man from his words speaking.

PEGEEN [*Going after him*] And you never went near to
see was he hurted or what ailed him at all?

SHAWN I did not, Pegeen Mike. It was a dark, lonesome
place to be hearing the like of him.

PEGEEN Well, you're a daring fellow, and if they find his
corpse stretched above in the dews of dawn, what'll
you say then to the peelers, or the Justice of the Peace?

SHAWN [*Thunderstruck*] I wasn't thinking of that. For
the love of God, Pegeen Mike, don't let on I was
speaking of him. Don't tell your father and the men
is coming above; for if they heard that story they'd
have great blabbing this night at the wake.

PEGEEN I'll maybe tell them, and I'll maybe not.

SHAWN They are coming at the door. Will you whisht,
I'm saying?

PEGEEN Whisht yourself.

[*She goes behind counter. Michael James, fat, jovial
publican, comes in followed by Philly Cullen,
who is thin and mistrusting, and Jimmy Farrell,
who is fat and amorous, about forty-five*]

MEN [*Together*] God bless you! The blessing of God on
this place!

PEGEEN God bless you kindly.

MICHAEL [*To men, who go to the counter*] Sit down now,

and take your rest. [*Crosses to Shawn at the fire*] And how is it you are, Shawn Keogh? Are you coming over the sands to Kate Cassidy's wake?

SHAWN I am not, Michael James. I'm going home the short cut to my bed.

PEGEEN [*Speaking across the counter*] He's right, too, and have you no shame, Michael James, to be quitting off for the whole night, and leaving myself lonesome in the shop?

MICHAEL [*Good-humouredly*] Isn't it the same whether I go for the whole night or a part only? and I'm thinking it's a queer daughter you are if you'd have me crossing backward through the Stooks of the Dead Women, with a drop taken.

PEGEEN If I am a queer daughter, it's a queer father'd be leaving me lonesome these twelve hours of dark, and I piling the turf with the dogs barking, and the calves mooing, and my own teeth rattling with the fear.

JIMMY [*Flatteringly*] What is there to hurt you, and you a fine, hardy girl would knock the heads of any two men in the place?

PEGEEN [*Working herself up*] Isn't there the harvest boys with their tongues red for drink, and the ten tinkers is camped in the east glen, and the thousand militia—bad cess to them!—walking idle through the land. There's lots surely to hurt me, and I won't stop alone in it, let himself do what he will.

MICHAEL If you're that afeard, let Shawn Keogh stop along with you. It's the will of God, I'm thinking, himself should be seeing to you now. [*They all turn on Shawn*]

SHAWN [*In horrified confusion*] I would and welcome, Michael James, but I'm afeard of Father Reilly; and

45

what at all would the Holy Father and the Cardinals of Rome be saying if they heard I did the like of that?

MICHAEL [*With contempt*] God help you! Can't you sit in by the hearth with the light lit and herself beyond in the room? You'll do that surely, for I've heard tell there's a queer fellow above, going mad or getting his death, maybe, in the gripe of the ditch, so she'd be safer this night with a person here.

SHAWN [*With plaintive despair*] I'm afeard of Father Reilly, I'm saying. Let you not be tempting me, and we near married itself.

PHILLY [*With cold contempt*] Lock him in the west room. He'll stay then and have no sin to be telling to the priest.

MICHAEL [*To Shawn, getting between him and the door*] Go up, now.

SHAWN [*At the top of his voice*] Don't stop me, Michael James. Let me out of the door, I'm saying, for the love of the Almighty God. Let me out. [*Trying to dodge past him*] Let me out of it, and may God grant you His indulgence in the hour of need.

MICHAEL [*Loudly*] Stop your noising, and sit down by the hearth. [*Gives him a push and goes to counter laughing*]

SHAWN [*Turning back, wringing his hands*] Oh, Father Reilly, and the saints of God, where will I hide myself today? Oh, St Joseph and St Patrick and St Brigid and St James, have mercy on me now!

[*Shawn turns round, sees door clear, and makes a rush for it*]

MICHAEL [*Catching him by the coat-tail*] You'd be going, is it?

SHAWN [*Screaming*] Leave me go, Michael James, leave

me go, you old Pagan, leave me go, or I'll get the curse of the priests on you, and of the scarlet-coated bishops of the Courts of Rome.

[*With a sudden movement he pulls himself out of his coat, and disappears out of the door, leaving his coat in Michael's hands*]

MICHAEL [*Turning round, and holding up coat*] Well, there's the coat of a Christian man. Oh, there's sainted glory this day in the lonesome west; and by the will of God I've got you a decent man, Pegeen, you'll have no call to be spying after if you've a score of young girls, maybe, weeding in your fields.

PEGEEN [*Taking up the defence of her property*] What right have you to be making game of a poor fellow for minding the priest, when it's your own the fault is, not paying a penny pot-boy to stand along with me and give me courage in the doing of my work.

[*She snaps the coat away from him, and goes behind counter with it*]

MICHAEL [*Taken aback*] Where would I get a pot-boy? Would you have me send the bell-man screaming in the streets of Castlebar?

SHAWN [*Opening the door a chink and putting in his head, in a small voice*] Michael James!

MICHAEL [*Imitating him*] What ails you?

SHAWN The queer dying fellow's beyond looking over the ditch. He's come up, I'm thinking, stealing your hens. [*Looks over his shoulder*] God help me, he's following me now [*he runs into room*], and if he's heard what I said, he'll be having my life, and I going home lonesome in the darkness of the night.

[*For a perceptible moment they watch the door with curiosity. Someone coughs outside. Then Christy*

47

*Mahon, a slight young man, comes in very tired
and frightened and dirty*]

CHRISTY [*In a small voice*] God save all here!

MEN God save you kindly!

CHRISTY [*Going to the counter*] I'd trouble you for a glass
of porter, woman of the house. [*He puts down coin*]

PEGEEN [*Serving him*] You're one of the tinkers, young
fellow, is beyond camped in the glen?

CHRISTY I am not; but I'm destroyed walking.

MICHAEL [*Patronizingly*] Let you come up then to the
fire. You're looking famished with the cold.

CHRISTY God reward you. [*He takes up his glass and goes
a little way across to the left, then stops and looks
about him*] Is it often the polis do be coming into this
place, master of the house?

MICHAEL If you'd come in better hours, you'd have seen
'Licensed for the Sale of Beer and Spirits, to be Con-
sumed on the Premises', written in white letters above
the door, and what would the polis want spying on me,
and not a decent house within four miles, the way every
living Christian is a bona fide, saving one widow alone?

CHRISTY [*With relief*] It's a safe house, so.

[*He goes over to the fire, sighing and moaning. Then
he sits down, putting his glass beside him, and
begins gnawing a turnip, too miserable to feel
the others staring at him with curiosity*]

MICHAEL [*Going after him*] Is it yourself is fearing the
polis? You're wanting, maybe?

CHRISTY There's many wanting.

MICHAEL Many, surely, with the broken harvest and the
ended wars. [*He picks up some stockings, etc., that are
near the fire, and carries them away furtively*] It
should be larceny, I'm thinking?

48

CHRISTY [*Dolefully*] I had it in my mind it was a different word and a bigger.

PEGEEN There's a queer lad. Were you never slapped in school, young fellow, that you don't know the name of your deed?

CHRISTY [*Bashfully*] I'm slow at learning, a middling scholar only.

MICHAEL If you're a dunce itself, you'd have a right to know that larceny's robbing and stealing. Is it for the like of that you're wanting?

CHRISTY [*With a flash of family pride*] And I the son of a strong farmer [*with a sudden qualm*], God rest his soul, could have bought up the whole of your old house a while since, from the butt of his tail-pocket, and not have missed the weight of it gone.

MICHAEL [*Impressed*] If it's not stealing, it's maybe something big.

CHRISTY [*Flattered*] Aye; it's maybe something big.

JIMMY He's a wicked-looking young fellow. Maybe he followed after a young woman on a lonesome night.

CHRISTY [*Shocked*] Oh, the saints forbid, mister; I was all times a decent lad.

PHILLY [*Turning on Jimmy*] You're a silly man, Jimmy Farrell. He said his father was a farmer a while since, and there's himself now in a poor state. Maybe the land was grabbed from him, and he did what any decent man would do.

MICHAEL [*To Christy, mysteriously*] Was it bailiffs?

CHRISTY The divil a one.

MICHAEL Agents?

CHRISTY The divil a one.

MICHAEL Landlords?

CHRISTY [*Peevishly*] Ah, not at all, I'm saying. You'd

see the like of them stories on any little paper of a Munster town. But I'm not calling to mind any person, gentle, simple, judge or jury, did the like of me.

[*They all draw nearer with delighted curiosity*]

PHILLY Well, that lad's a puzzle-the-world.

JIMMY He'd beat Dan Davies's circus, or the holy missioners making sermons on the villainy of man. Try him again, Philly.

PHILLY Did you strike golden guineas out of solder, young fellow, or shilling coins itself?

CHRISTY I did not, mister, not sixpence nor a farthing coin.

JIMMY Did you marry three wives maybe? I'm told there's a sprinkling have done that among the holy Luthers of the preaching north.

CHRISTY [*Shyly*] I never married with one, let alone with a couple or three.

PHILLY Maybe he went fighting for the Boers, the like of the man beyond, was judged to be hanged, quartered, and drawn. Were you off east, young fellow, fighting bloody wars for Kruger and the freedom of the Boers?

CHRISTY I never left my own parish till Tuesday was a week.

PEGEEN [*Coming from counter*] He's done nothing, so. [*To Christy*] If you didn't commit murder or a bad, nasty thing; or false coining, or robbery, or butchery, or the like of them, there isn't anything that would be worth your troubling for to run from now. You did nothing at all.

CHRISTY [*His feelings hurt*] That's an unkindly thing to be saying to a poor orphaned traveller, has a prison behind him, and hanging before, and hell's gap gaping below.

PEGEEN [*With a sign to the men to be quiet*] You're only saying it. You did nothing at all. A soft lad the like of you wouldn't slit the wind pipe of a screeching sow.

CHRISTY [*Offended*] You're not speaking the truth.

PEGEEN [*In mock rage*] Not speaking the truth, is it? Would you have me knock the head of you with the butt of the broom?

CHRISTY [*Twisting round on her with a sharp cry of horror*] Don't strike me. I killed my poor father, Tuesday was a week, for doing the like of that.

PEGEEN [*With blank amazement*] Is it killed your father?

CHRISTY [*Subsiding*] With the help of God I did, surely, and that the Holy Immaculate Mother may intercede for his soul.

PHILLY [*Retreating with Jimmy*] There's a daring fellow.

JIMMY Oh, glory be to God!

MICHAEL [*With great respect*] That was a hanging crime, mister honey. You should have had good reason for doing the like of that.

CHRISTY [*In a very reasonable tone*] He was a dirty man, God forgive him, and he getting old and crusty, the way I couldn't put up with him at all.

PEGEEN And you shot him dead?

CHRISTY [*Shaking his head*] I never used weapons. I've no licence, and I'm a law-fearing man.

MICHAEL It was with a hilted knife maybe? I'm told, in the big world, it's bloody knives they use.

CHRISTY [*Loudly, scandalized*] Do you take me for a slaughter-boy?

PEGEEN You never hanged him, the way Jimmy Farrell hanged his dog from the licence, and had it screeching and wriggling three hours at the butt of a string, and himself swearing it was a dead dog, and the peelers swearing it had life?

CHRISTY I did not, then. I just riz the loy and let fall the edge of it on the ridge of his skull, and he went down at my feet like an empty sack, and never let a grunt or groan from him at all.

MICHAEL [Making a sign to Pegeen to fill Christy's glass] And what way weren't you hanged, mister? Did you bury him then?

CHRISTY [Considering] Aye. I buried him then. Wasn't I digging spuds in the field?

MICHAEL And the peelers never followed after you the eleven days that you're out?

CHRISTY [Shaking his head] Never a one of them, and I walking forward facing hog, dog, or divil on the high-way of the road.

PHILLY [Nodding wisely] It's only with a common week-day kind of murderer them lads would be trusting their carcass, and that man should be a great terror when his temper's roused.

MICHAEL He should then. [To Christy] And where was it, mister honey, that you did the deed?

CHRISTY [Looking at him with suspicion] Oh, a distant place, master of the house, a windy corner of high, distant hills.

PHILLY [Nodding with approval] He's a close man, and he's right, surely.

PEGEEN That'd be a lad with the sense of Solomon to have for a pot-boy, Michael James, if it's the truth you're seeking one at all.

PHILLY The peelers is fearing him, and if you'd that lad in the house there isn't one of them would come smelling around if the dogs itself were lapping poteen from the dung-pit of the yard.

JIMMY Bravery's a treasure in a lonesome place. and a lad would kill his father, I'm thinking, would face a foxy divil with a pitchpike on the flags of hell.

PEGEEN It's the truth they're saying, and if I'd that lad in the house, I wouldn't be fearing the loosèd khaki cut-throats, or the walking dead.

CHRISTY [*Swelling with surprise and triumph*] Well, glory be to God!

MICHAEL [*With deference*] Would you think well to stop here and be pot-boy, mister honey, if we gave you good wages, and didn't destroy you with the weight of work.

SHAWN [*Coming forward uneasily*] That'd be a queer kind to bring into a decent, quiet household with the like of Pegeen Mike.

PEGEEN [*Very sharply*] Will you whisht? Who's speaking to you?

SHAWN [*Retreating*] A bloody-handed murderer the like of . . .

PEGEEN [*Snapping at him*] Whisht, I am saying; we'll take no fooling from your like at all. [*To Christy, with a honeyed voice*] And you, young fellow, you'd have a right to stop, I'm thinking, for we'd do our all and utmost to content your needs.

CHRISTY [*Overcome with wonder*] And I'd be safe this place from the searching law?

MICHAEL You would, surely. If they're not fearing you, itself, the peelers in this place is decent, drouthy poor fellows, wouldn't touch a cur dog and not give warning in the dead of night.

PEGEEN [*Very kindly and persuasively*] Let you stop a short while anyhow. Aren't you destroyed by walking

with your feet in bleeding blisters, and your whole
skin needing washing like a Wicklow sheep.

CHRISTY [*Looking round with satisfaction*] It's a nice
room, and if it's not humbugging me you are, I'm
thinking that I'll surely stay.

JIMMY [*Jumps up*] Now, by the grace of God, herself
will be safe this night, with a man killed his father
holding danger from the door, and let you come on,
Michael James, or they'll have the best stuff drunk
at the wake.

MICHAEL [*Going to the door with men*] And begging
your pardon, mister, what name will we call you, for
we'd like to know?

CHRISTY Christopher Mahon

MICHAEL Well, God bless you, Christy, and a good rest
till we meet again when the sun'll be rising to the
noon of the day.

CHRISTY God bless you all.

MEN God bless you.

[*They go out, except Shawn, who lingers at the door*]

SHAWN [*To Pegeen*] Are you wanting me to stop along
with you and keep you from harm?

PEGEEN [*Gruffly*] Didn't you say you were fearing Father
Reilly?

SHAWN There'd be no harm staying now, I'm thinking,
and himself in it too.

PEGEEN You wouldn't stay when there was need for you,
and let you step off nimble this time when there's none.

SHAWN Didn't I say it was Father Reilly. . . .

PEGEEN Go on, then, to Father Reilly [*in a jeering tone*],
and let him put you in the holy brotherhoods, and
leave that lad to me.

SHAWN If I meet the Widow Quin . . .

PEGEEN Go on, I'm saying, and don't be waking this place with your noise. [*She hustles him out and bolts door*] That lad would wear the spirits from the saints of peace. [*Bustles about, then takes off her apron and pins it up in the window as a blind, Christy watching her timidly. Then she comes to him and speaks with bland good humour*] Let you stretch out now by the fire, young fellow. You should be destroyed travelling.

CHRISTY [*Shyly again, drawing off his boots*] I'm tired surely, walking wild eleven days, and waking fearful in the night.

[*He holds up one of his feet, feeling his blisters, and looking at them with compassion*]

PEGEEN [*Standing beside him, watching him with delight*] You should have had great people in your family, I'm thinking, with the little, small feet you have, and you with a kind of a quality name, the like of what you'd find on the great powers and potentates of France and Spain.

CHRISTY [*With pride*] We were great, surely, with wide and windy acres of rich Munster land.

PEGEEN Wasn't I telling you, and you a fine, handsome young fellow with a noble brow?

CHRISTY [*With a flush of delighted surprise*] Is it me?

PEGEEN Aye. Did you never hear that from the young girls where you come from in the west or south?

CHRISTY [*With venom*] I did not, then. Oh, they're bloody liars in the naked parish where I grew a man.

PEGEEN If they are itself, you've heard it these days, I'm thinking, and you walking the world telling out your story to young girls or old.

CHRISTY I've told my story no place till this night, Pegeen Mike, and it's foolish I was here, maybe, to be talking free; but you're decent people, I'm thinking, and yourself a kindly woman, the way I wasn't fearing you at all.

PEGEEN [*Filling a sack with straw*] You've said the like of that, maybe, in every cot and cabin where you've met a young girl on your way.

CHRISTY [*Going over to her, gradually raising his voice*] I've said it nowhere till this night, I'm telling you; for I've seen none the like of you the eleven long days I am walking the world, looking over a low ditch or a high ditch on my north or south, into stony, scattered fields, or scribes of bog, where you'd see young, limber girls, and fine, prancing women making laughter with the men.

PEGEEN If you weren't destroyed travelling, you'd have as much talk and streeleen, I'm thinking, as Owen Roe O'Sullivan or the poets of the Dingle Bay; and I've heard all times it's the poets are your like—fine, fiery fellows with great rages when their temper's roused.

CHRISTY [*Drawing a little nearer to her*] You've a power of rings, God bless you, and would there be any offence if I was asking are you single now?

PEGEEN What would I want wedding so young?

CHRISTY [*With relief*] We're alike so.

PEGEEN [*She puts sack on settle and beats it up*] I never killed my father. I'd be afeared to do that, except I was the like of yourself with blind rages tearing me within, for I'm thinking you should have had great tussling when the end was come.

CHRISTY [*Expanding with delight at the first confidential talk he has ever had with a woman*] We had not then. It was a hard woman was come over the hill; and if he

56

was always a crusty kind, when he'd a hard woman setting him on, not the divil himself or his four fathers could put up with him at all.

PEGEEN [*With curiosity*] And isn't it a great wonder that one wasn't fearing you?

CHRISTY [*Very confidentially*] Up to the day I killed my father, there wasn't a person in Ireland knew the kind I was, and I there drinking, waking, eating, sleeping, a quiet, simple poor fellow with no man giving me heed.

PEGEEN [*Getting a quilt out of cupboard and putting it on the sack*] It was the girls were giving you heed, maybe, and I'm thinking it's most conceit you'd have to be gaming with their like.

CHRISTY [*Shaking his head with simplicity*] Not the girls itself, and I won't tell you a lie. There wasn't any one heeding me in that place saving only the dumb beasts of the field.

[*He sits down at fire*]

PEGEEN [*With disappointment*] And I thinking you should have been living the like of a king of Norway or the eastern world.

[*She comes and sits beside him after placing bread and mug of milk on the table*]

CHRISTY [*Laughing piteously*] The like of a king, is it? And I after toiling, moiling, digging, dodging from the dawn till dusk; with never a sight of joy or sport saving only when I'd be abroad in the dark night poaching rabbits on hills, for I was a divil to poach, God forgive me [*very naïvely*], and I near got six months for going with a dung fork and stabbing a fish.

PEGEEN And it's that you'd call sport, is it, to be abroad in the darkness with yourself alone?

CHRISTY I did, God help me, and there I'd be as happy as the sunshine of St. Martin's Day, watching the light passing the north or the patches of fog, till I'd hear a rabbit starting to screech and I'd go running in the furze. Then, when I'd my full share, I'd come walking down where you'd see the ducks and geese stretched sleeping on the highway of the road, and before I'd pass the dunghill, I'd hear himself snoring out—a loud, lonesome snore he'd be making all times, the while he was sleeping; and he a man'd be raging all times, the while he was waking, like a gaudy officer you'd hear cursing and damning and swearing oaths.

PEGEEN Providence and Mercy, spare us all!

CHRISTY It's that you'd say surely if you seen him and he after drinking for weeks, rising up in the red dawn, or before it maybe, and going out into the yard as naked as an ash-tree in the moon of May, and shying clods against the visage of the stars till he'd put the fear of death into the banbhs and the screeching sows.

PEGEEN I'd be well-nigh afeard of that lad myself, I'm thinking. And there was no one in it but the two of you alone?

CHRISTY The divil a one, though he'd sons and daughters walking all great states and territories of the world, and not a one of them, to this day, but would say their seven curses on him, and they rousing up to let a cough or sneeze, maybe, in the deadness of the night.

PEGEEN [*Nodding her head*] Well, you should have been a queer lot. I never cursed my father the like of that, though I'm twenty and more years of age.

CHRISTY Then you'd have cursed mine, I'm telling you, and he a man never gave peace to any, saving when he'd get two months or three, or be locked in the asylums for battering peelers or assaulting men [*with depression*], the way it was a bitter life he led me till I did up a Tuesday and halve his skull.

PEGEEN [*Putting her hand on his shoulder*] Well, you'll have peace in this place, Christy Mahon, and none to trouble you, and it's near time a fine lad like you should have your good share of the earth.

CHRISTY It's time surely, and I a seemly fellow with great strength in me and bravery of . . .

[*Someone knocks*]

CHRISTY [*Clinging to Pegeen*] Oh, glory! it's late for knocking, and this last while I'm in terror of the peelers, and the walking dead.

[*Knocking again*]

PEGEEN Who's there?

VOICE [*Outside*] Me.

PEGEEN Who's me?

VOICE The Widow Quin.

PEGEEN [*Jumping up and giving him the bread and milk*] Go on now with your supper, and let on to be sleepy, for if she found you were such a warrant to talk, she'd be stringing gabble till the dawn of day.

[*He takes bread and sits shyly with his back to the door*]

PEGEEN [*Opening door, with temper*] What ails you, or what is it you're wanting at this hour of the night?

WIDOW QUIN [*Coming in a step and peering at Christy*] I'm after meeting Shawn Keogh and Father Reilly below, who told me of your curiosity man, and they fearing by this time he was roaring, romping on your hands with drink.

PEGEEN [*Pointing to Christy*] Look now is he roaring, and he stretched out drowsy with his supper and his

59

mug of milk. Walk down and tell that to Father Reilly
and to Shaneen Keogh.

WIDOW QUIN [Coming forward] I'll not see them again,
for I've their word to lead that lad forward to lodge
with me.

PEGEEN [In blank amazement] This night is it?

WIDOW QUIN [Going over] This night. 'It isn't fitting,'
says the priesteen, 'to have his likeness lodging with an
orphaned girl.' [To Christy] God save you mister!

CHRISTY [Shyly] God save you kindly!

WIDOW QUIN [Looking at him with half amused curiosity]
Well, aren't you a little smiling fellow? It should have
been great and bitter torments did rouse your spirits to
a deed of blood.

CHRISTY [Doubtfully] It should, maybe.

WIDOW QUIN It's more than 'maybe' I'm saying, and it'd
soften my heart to see you sitting so simple with your
cup and cake, and you fitter to be saying your catechism than slaying your da.

PEGEEN [At counter, washing glasses] There's talking
when any'd see he's fit to be holding his head high with
the wonders of the world. Walk on from this, for I'll
not have him tormented, and he destroyed travelling
since Tuesday was a week.

WIDOW QUIN [Peaceably] We'll be walking surely when
his supper's done, and you'll find we're great company,
young fellow, when it's of the like of you and me
you'd hear the penny poets singing in an August Fair.

CHRISTY [Innocently] Did you kill your father?

PEGEEN [Contemptuously] She did not. She hit himself
with a worn pick, and the rusted poison did corrode
his blood the way he never overed it, and died after.
That was a sneaky kind of murder did win small glory

with the boys itself.

[*She crosses to Christy's left*]

WIDOW QUIN [*With good humour*] If it didn't, maybe all knows a widow woman has buried her children and destroyed her man is a wiser comrade for a young lad than a girl, the like of you, who'd go helter-skeltering after any man would let you a wink upon the road.

PEGEEN [*Breaking out into wild rage*] And you'll say that, Widow Quin, and you gasping with the rage you had racing the hill beyond to look on his face.

WIDOW QUIN [*Laughing derisively*] Me, is it? Well, Father Reilly has cuteness to divide you now. [*She pulls Christy up*] There's great temptation in a man did slay his da, and we'd best be going, young fellow; so rise up and come with me.

PEGEEN [*Seizing his arm*] He'll not stir. He's pot-boy in this place, and I'll not have him stolen off and kidnapped while himself's abroad.

WIDOW QUIN It'd be a crazy pot-boy'd lodge him in the shebeen where he works by day, so you'd have a right to come on, young fellow, till you see my little houscen, a perch off on the rising hill.

PEGEEN Wait till morning, Christy Mahon. Wait till you lay eyes on her leaky thatch is growing more pasture for her buck goat than her square of fields, and she without a tramp itself to keep in order her place at all.

WIDOW QUIN When you see me contriving in my little gardens, Christy Mahon, you'll swear the Lord God formed me to be living lone, and that there isn't my match in Mayo for thatching, or mowing, or shearing a sheep.

PEGEEN [*With noisy scorn*] It's true the Lord God formed you to contrive indeed. Doesn't the world know you

reared a black ram at your own breast, so that the Lord
Bishop of Connaught felt the elements of a Christian,
and he eating it after in a kidney stew? Doesn't the
world know you've been seen shaving the foxy skipper
from France for a threepenny-bit and a sop of grass
tobacco would wring the liver from a mountain goat
you'd meet leaping the hills?

WIDOW QUIN [*With amusement*] Do you hear her now,
young fellow? Do you hear the way she'll be rating
at your own self when a week is by?

PEGEEN [*To Christy*] Don't heed her. Tell her to go on
into her pigsty and not plague us here.

WIDOW QUIN I'm going; but he'll come with me.

PEGEEN [*Shaking him*] Are you dumb, young fellow?

CHRISTY [*Timidly to Widow Quin*] God increase you;
but I'm pot-boy in this place, and it's here I liefer stay.

PEGEEN [*Triumphantly*] Now you have heard him, and
go on from this.

WIDOW QUIN [*Looking round the room*] It's lonesome this
hour crossing the hill, and if he won't come along with
me, I'd have a right maybe to stop this night with
yourselves. Let me stretch out on the settle, Pegeen
Mike; and himself can lie by the hearth.

PEGEEN [*Short and fiercely*] Faith, I won't. Quit off or
I will send you now.

WIDOW QUIN [*Gathering her shawl up*] Well, it's a terror
to be aged a score. [*To Christy*] God bless you now,
young fellow, and let you be wary, or there's right
torment will await you here if you go romancing with
her like, and she waiting only, as they bade me say,
on a sheepskin parchment to be wed with Shawn
Keogh of Killakeen.

CHRISTY [*Going to Pegeen as she bolts door*] What's that

she's after saying?

PEGEEN Lies and blather, you've no call to mind. Well, isn't Shawn Keogh an impudent fellow to send up spying on me? Wait till I lay hands on him. Let him wait, I'm saying.

CHRISTY And you're not wedding him at all?

PEGEEN I wouldn't wed him if a bishop came walking for to join us here.

CHRISTY That God in glory may be thanked for that.

PEGEEN There's your bed now. I've put a quilt upon you I'm after quilting a while since with my own two hands, and you'd best stretch out now for your sleep, and may God give you a good rest till I call you in the morning when the cocks will crow.

CHRISTY [*As she goes to inner room*] May God and Mary and St. Patrick bless you and reward you for your kindly talk. [*She shuts the door behind her. He settles his bed slowly, feeling the quilt with immense satisfaction*] Well, it's a clean bed and soft with it, and it's great luck and company I've won me in the end of time—two fine women fighting for the likes of me—till I'm thinking this night wasn't I a foolish fellow not to kill my father in the years gone by.

CURTAIN

ACT II

Scene as before. Brilliant morning light. Christy, looking bright and cheerful, is cleaning a girl's boots.

CHRISTY [*To himself, counting jugs on dresser*] Half a hundred beyond. Ten there. A score that's above. Eighty jugs. Six cups and a broken one. Two plates. A power of glasses. Bottles, a schoolmaster'd be hard set to count, and enough in them, I'm thinking, to drunken all the wealth and wisdom of the county Clare. [*He puts down the boot carefully*] There's her boots now, nice and decent for her evening use, and isn't it grand brushes she has? [*He puts them down and goes by degrees to the looking-glass*] Well, this'd be a fine place to be my whole life talking out with swearing Christians, in place of my old dogs and cat; and I stalking around, smoking my pipe and drinking my fill, and never a day's work but drawing a cork an odd time, or wiping a glass, or rinsing out a shiny tumbler for a decent man. [*He takes the looking-glass from the wall and puts it on the back of a chair; then sits down in front of it and begins washing his face*] Didn't I know rightly, I was handsome, though it was the divil's own mirror we had beyond, would twist a squint across an angel's brow; and I'll be growing fine from this day, the way I'll have a soft lovely skin on me and won't be the like of the clumsy young fellows do be ploughing all times in the earth and dung. [*He starts*] Is she coming again? [*He looks out*] Stranger

64

girls. God help me, where'll I hide myself away and
my long neck naked to the world? [*He looks out*] I'd
best go to the room maybe till I'm dressed again.

> [*He gathers up his coat and the looking-glass, and
> runs into the inner room. The door is pushed
> open, and Susan Brady looks in, and knocks on
> door*]

SUSAN There's nobody in it. [*Knocks again*]

NELLY [*Pushing her in and following her, with Honor
Blake and Sara Tansey*] It'd be early for them both to
be out walking the hill.

SUSAN I'm thinking Shawn Keogh was making game of
us, and there's no such man in it at all.

HONOR [*Pointing to straw and quilt*] Look at that. He's
been sleeping there in the night. Well, it'll be a hard
case if he's gone off now, the way we'll never set our
eyes on a man killed his father, and we after rising
early and destroying ourselves running fast on the hill.

NELLY Are you thinking them's his boots?

SARAH [*Taking them up*] If they are, there should be his
father's track on them. Did you never read in the
papers the way murdered men do bleed and drip?

SUSAN Is that blood there, Sara Tansey?

SARA [*Smelling it*] That's bog water, I'm thinking; but
it's his own they are, surely, for I never seen the like
of them for whitey mud, and red mud, and turf on
them, and the fine sands of the sea. That man's been
walking, I'm telling you.

> [*She goes down right, putting on one of his boots*]

SUSAN [*Going to window*] Maybe he's stolen off to Belmullet with the boots of Michael James, and you'd
have a right so to follow after him, Sara Tansey, and
you the one yoked the ass-cart and drove ten miles to

set your eyes on the man bit the yellow lady's nostril on the northern shore. [*She looks out*]

SARA [*Running to window, with one boot on*] Don't be talking, and we fooled today. [*Putting on the other boot*] There's a pair do fit me well and I'll be keeping them for walking to the priest, when you'd be ashamed this place, going up winter and summer with nothing worth while to confess at all.

HONOR [*Who has been listening at door*] Whisht! there's someone inside the room. [*She pushes door a chink open*] It's a man.

[*Sara kicks off boots and puts them where they were. They all stand in a line looking through chink*]

SARA I'll call him. Mister! Mister! [*He puts in his head*] Is Pegeen within?

CHRISTY [*Coming in as meek as a mouse, with the looking-glass held behind his back*] She's above on the cnuceen, seeking the nanny goats, the way she'd have a sup of goats' milk for to colour my tea.

SARA And asking your pardon, is it you's the man killed his father?

CHRISTY [*Sidling toward the nail where the glass was hanging*] I am, God help me!

SARA [*Taking eggs she has brought*] Then my thousand welcomes to you, and I've run up with a brace of duck's eggs for your food today. Pegeen's ducks is no use, but these are the real rich sort. Hold out your hand and you'll see it's no lie I'm telling you.

CHRISTY [*Coming foward shyly, and holding out his left hand*] They're a great and weighty size.

SUSAN And I run up with a pat of butter, for it'd be a poor thing to have you eating your spuds dry, and you after running a great way since you did destroy your da.

CHRISTY Thank you kindly.

HONOR And I brought you a little cut of a cake, for you should have a thin stomach on you, and you that length walking the world.

NELLY And I brought you a little laying pullet—boiled and all she is—was crushed at the fall of night by the curate's car. Feel the fat of the breast, mister.

CHRISTY It's bursting, surely.

[*He feels it with the back of his hand, in which he holds the presents*]

SARA Will you pinch it? Is your right hand too sacred for to use at all? [*She slips round behind him*] It's a glass he has. Well, I never seen to this day a man with a looking-glass held to his back. Them that kills their fathers is a vain lot surely. [*Girls giggle*]

CHRISTY [*Smiling innocently and piling presents on glass*] I'm very thankful to you all today. . . .

WIDOW QUIN [*Coming in quietly, at door*] Sara Tansey, Susan Brady, Honor Blake! What in glory has you here at this hour of day!

GIRLS [*Giggling*] That's the man killed his father.

WIDOW QUIN [*Coming to them*] I know well it's the man; and I'm after putting him down in the sports below for racing, leaping, pitching, and the Lord knows what.

SARA [*Exuberantly*] That's right, Widow Quin. I'll bet my dowry that he'll lick the world.

WIDOW QUIN If you will, you'd have a right to have him fresh and nourished in place of nursing a feast. [*Taking presents*] Are you fasting or fed, young fellow?

CHRISTY Fasting, if you please.

WIDOW QUIN [*Loudly*] Well, you're the lot. Stir up now and give him his breakfast. [*To Christy*] Come here

67

to me [*she puts him on bench beside her while the girls make tea and get his breakfast*], and let you tell us your story before Pegeen will come, in place of grinning your ears off like the moon of May.

CHRISTY [*Beginning to be pleased*] It's a long story; you'd be destroyed listening.

WIDOW QUIN Don't be letting on to be shy, a fine, gamy, treacherous lad the like of you. Was it in your house beyond you cracked his skull?

CHRISTY [*Shy but flattered*] It was not. We were digging spuds in his cold, sloping, stony, divil's patch of a field.

WIDOW QUIN And you went asking money of him, or making talk of getting a wife would drive him from his farm?

CHRISTY I did not, then; but there I was, digging and digging, and 'You squinting idot,' says he, 'let you walk down now and tell the priest you'll wed the Widow Casey in a score of days.'

WIDOW QUIN And what kind was she?

CHRISTY [*With horror*] A walking terror from beyond the hills, and she two score and five years, and two hundred weights and five pounds in the weighing scales, with a limping leg on her, and a blinded eye, and she a woman of noted misbehaviour with the old and young.

GIRLS [*Clustering round him, serving him*] Glory be.

WIDOW QUIN And what did he want driving you to wed with her? [*She takes a bit of the chicken*]

CHRISTY [*Eating with growing satisfaction*] He was letting on I was wanting a protector from the harshness of the world, and he without a thought the whole while but how he'd have her hut to live in and her gold to drink.

WIDOW QUIN There's maybe worse than a dry hearth and a widow woman and your glass at night. So you hit him then?

CHRISTY [*Getting almost excited*] I did not. 'I won't wed her,' says I, 'when all know she did suckle me for six weeks when I came into the world, and she a hag this day with a tongue on her has the crows and seabirds scattered, the way they wouldn't cast a shadow on her garden with the dread of her curse.'

WIDOW QUIN [*Teasingly*] That one should be right company.

SARA [*Eagerly*] Don't mind her. Did you kill him then?

CHRISTY 'She's too good for the like of you,' says he, 'and go on now or I'll flatten you out like a crawling beast has passed under a dray.' 'You will not if I can help it,' says I. 'Go on,' says he, 'or I'll have the divil making garters of your limbs tonight.' 'You will not if I can help it,' says I. [*He sits up brandishing his mug*]

SARA You were right surely.

CHRISTY [*Impressively*] With that the sun came out between the cloud and the hill, and it shining green in my face. 'God have mercy on your soul,' says he, lifting a scythe. 'Or on your own,' says I, raising the loy.

SUSAN That's a grand story.

HONOR He tells it lovely.

CHRISTY [*Flattered and confident, waving bone*] He gave a drive with the scythe, and I gave a lep to the east. Then I turned around with my back to the north, and I hit a blow on the ridge of his skull, laid him stretched out, and he split to the knob of his gullet.

[*He raises the chicken bone to his Adam's apple*]

GIRLS [*Together*] Well, you're a marvel! Oh, God bless you! You're the lad, surely!

SUSAN I'm thinking the Lord God sent him this road to make a second husband to the Widow Quin, and she with a great yearning to be wedded, though all dread her here. Lift him on her knee, Sara Tansey.

WIDOW QUIN Don't tease him.

SARA [*Going over to dresser and counter very quickly and getting two glasses and porter*] You're heroes, surely, and let you drink a supeen with your arms linked like the outlandish lovers in the sailor's song. [*She links their arms and gives them the glasses*] There now. Drink a health to the wonders of the western world, the pirates, preachers, poteen-makers, with the jobbing jockies; parching peelers, and the juries fill their stomachs selling judgments of the English law. [*Brandishing the bottle*]

WIDOW QUIN That's a right toast, Sara Tansey. Now, Christy.

[*They drink with their arms linked, he drinking with his left hand, she with her right. As they are drinking, Pegeen Mike comes in with a milk-can and stands aghast. They all spring away from Christy. He goes down left. Widow Quin remains seated*]

PEGEEN [*Angrily to Sara*] What is it you're wanting?

SARA [*Twisting her apron*] An ounce of tobacco.

PEGEEN Have you tuppence?

SARA I've forgotten my purse.

PEGEEN Then you'd best be getting it and not be fooling us here. [*To the Widow Quin, with more elaborate scorn*] And what is it you're wanting, Widow Quin?

WIDOW QUIN [*Insolently*] A penn'orth of starch.

PEGEEN [*Breaking out*] And you without a white shift or a shirt in your whole family since the dying of the flood. I've no starch for the like of you, and let you walk on now to Killamuck.

WIDOW QUIN [*Turning to Christy, as she goes out with the girls*] Well, you're mighty huffy this day, Pegeen Mike, and you, young fellow, let you not forget the sports and racing when the noon is by. [*They go out*]

PEGEEN [*Imperiously*] Fling out that rubbish and put them cups away. [*Christy tidies away in great haste*] Shove in the bench by the wall. [*He does so*] And hang that glass on the nail. What disturbed it at all?

CHRISTY [*Very meekly*] I was making myself decent only, and this a fine country for young lovely girls.

PEGEEN [*Sharply*] Whisht your talking of girls. [*Goes to counter on right*]

CHRISTY Wouldn't any wish to be decent in a place . . .

PEGEEN Whisht, I'm saying.

CHRISTY [*Looks at her face for a moment with great misgivings, then as a last effort takes up a loy, and goes towards her, with feigned assurance*] It was with a loy the like of that I killed my father.

PEGEEN [*Still sharply*] You've told me that story six times since the dawn of day.

CHRISTY [*Reproachfully*] It's a queer thing you wouldn't care to be hearing it and them girls after walking four miles to be listening to me now.

PEGEEN [*Turning round astonished*] Four miles?

CHRISTY [*Apologetically*] Didn't himself say there were only bona fides living in the place?

PEGEEN It's bona fides by the road they are, but that lot came over the river lepping the stones. It's not three perches when you go like that, and I was down this morning looking on the papers the post-boy does have in his bag. [*With meaning and emphasis*] For there

71

was great news this day, Christopher Mahon. [*She goes into room on left*]

CHRISTY [*Suspiciously*] Is it news of my murder?

PEGEEN [*Inside*] Murder, indeed.

CHRISTY [*Loudly*] A murdered da?

PEGEEN [*Coming in again and crossing right*] There was not, but a story filled half a page of the hanging of a man. Ah, that should be a fearful end, young fellow, and it worst of all for a man destroyed his da; for the like of him would get small mercies, and when it's dead he is they'd put him in a narrow grave, with cheap sacking wrapping him round, and pour down quick-lime on his head, the way you'd see a woman pouring any frish-frash from a cup.

CHRISTY [*Very miserably*] Oh, God help me. Are you thinking I'm safe? You were saying at the fall of night I was shut of jeopardy and I here with yourselves.

PEGEEN [*Severely*] You'll be shut of jeopardy no place if you go talking with a pack of wild girls the like of them do be walking abroad with the peelers, talking whispers at the fall of night.

CHRISTY [*With terror*] And you're thinking they'd tell?

PEGEEN [*With mock sympathy*] Who knows, God help you?

CHRISTY [*Loudly*] What joy would they have to bring hanging to the likes of me?

PEGEEN It's queer joys they have, and who knows the thing they'd do, if it'd make the green stones cry itself to think of you swaying and swinging at the butt of a rope, and you with a fine, stout neck, God bless you! the way you'd be a half an hour, in great anguish, getting your death.

CHRISTY [*Getting his boots and putting them on*] If there's that terror of them, it'd be best, maybe, I went on wandering like Esau or Cain and Abel on the sides of Neifin or the Erris plain.

PEGEEN [*Beginning to play with him*] It would, maybe, for I've heard the circuit judges this place is a heartless crew.

CHRISTY [*Bitterly*] It's more than judges this place is a heartless crew. [*Looking up at her*] And isn't it a poor thing to be starting again, and I a lonesome fellow will be looking out on women and girls the way the needy fallen spirits do be looking on the Lord?

PEGEEN What call have you to be that lonesome when there's poor girls walking Mayo in their thousands now?

CHRISTY [*Grimly*] It's well you know what call I have. It's well you know it's a lonesome thing to be passing small towns with the lights shining sideways when the night is down, or going in strange places with a dog noising before you and a dog noising behind, or drawn to the cities where you'd hear a voice kissing and talking deep love in every shadow of the ditch, and you passing on with an empty, hungry stomach failing from your heart.

PEGEEN I'm thinking you're an odd man, Christy Mahon. The oddest walking fellow I ever set my eyes on to this hour today.

CHRISTY What would any be but odd men and they living lonesome in the world?

PEGEEN I'm not odd, and I'm my whole life with my father only.

CHRISTY [*With infinite admiration*] How would a lovely, handsome woman the like of you be lonesome when all men should be thronging around to hear the sweet-

73

ness of your voice, and the little infant children should
be pestering your steps, I'm thinking, and you walking
the roads.

PEGEEN I'm hard set to know what way a coaxing fellow
the like of yourself should be lonesome either.

CHRISTY Coaxing?

PEGEEN Would you have me think a man never talked
with the girls would have the words you've spoken today? It's only letting on you are to be lonesome, the
way you'd get around me now.

CHRISTY I wish to God I was letting on; but I was lonesome all times, and born lonesome, I'm thinking, as the
moon of dawn.

[*Going to door*]

PEGEEN [*Puzzled by his talk*] Well, it's a story I'm not
understanding at all why you'd be worse than another,
Christy Mahon, and you a fine lad with the great
savagery to destroy your da.

CHRISTY It's little I'm understanding myself, saving only
that my heart's scalded this day, and I going off stretching out the earth between us, the way I'll not be
waking near you another dawn of the year till the two
of us do arise to hope or judgment with the saints of
God, and now I'd best be going with my wattle in my
hand, for hanging is a poor thing [*turning to go*], and
it's little welcome only is left me in this house today.

PEGEEN [*Sharply*] Christy. [*He turns round*] Come here
to me. [*He goes towards her*] Lay down that switch
and throw some sods on the fire. You're pot-boy in
this place, and I'll not have you mitch off from us now.

CHRISTY You were saying I'd be hanged if I stay.

PEGEEN [*Quite kindly at last*] I'm after going down and
reading the fearful crimes of Ireland for two weeks or

three, and there wasn't a word of your murder. [*Getting up and going over to the counter*] They've likely not found the body. You're safe so with ourselves.

CHRISTY [*Astonished, slowly*] It's making game of me you were [*following her with fearful joy*], and I can stay so, working at your side, and I not lonesome from this mortal day.

PEGEEN What's to hinder you staying, except the widow woman or the young girls would inveigle you off?

CHRISTY [*With rapture*] And I'll have your words from this day filling my ears, and that look is come upon you meeting my two eyes, and I watching you loafing around in the warm sun, or rinsing your ankles when the night is come.

PEGEEN [*Kindly, but a little embarrassed*] I'm thinking you'll be a loyal young lad to have working around, and if you vexed me a while since with your leaguing with the girls, I wouldn't give a thraneen for a lad hadn't a mighty spirit in him and a gamy heart.

[*Shawn Keogh runs in carrying a cleeve on his back, followed by the Widow Quin*]

SHAWN [*To Pegeen*] I was passing below, and I seen your mountainy sheep eating cabbages in Jimmy's field. Run up or they'll be bursting surely.

PEGEEN Oh, God mend them!

[*She puts a shawl over her head and runs out*]

CHRISTY [*Looking from one to the other. Still in high spirits*] I'd best go to her aid maybe. I'm handy with ewes.

WIDOW QUIN [*Closing the door*] She can do that much, and there is Shaneen has long speeches for to tell you now. [*She sits down with an amused smile*]

SHAWN [*Taking something from his pocket and offering it to Christy*] Do you see that, mister?

CHRISTY [*Looking at it*] The half of a ticket to the Western States!

SHAWN [*Trembling with anxiety*] I'll give it to you and my new hat [*pulling it out of hamper*]; and my breeches with the double seat [*pulling it out*]; and my new coat is woven from the blackest shearings for three miles around [*giving him the coat*]; I'll give you the whole of them, and my blessing, and the blessing of Father Reilly itself, maybe, if you'll quit from this and leave us in the peace we had till last night at the fall of dark.

CHRISTY [*With a new arrogance*] And for what is it you're wanting to get shut of me?

SHAWN [*Looking to the Widow for help*] I'm a poor scholar with middling faculties to coin a lie, so I'll tell you the truth, Christy Mahon. I'm wedding with Pegeen beyond, and I don't think well of having a clever fearless man the like of you dwelling in her house.

CHRISTY [*Almost pugnaciously*] And you'd be using bribery for to banish me?

SHAWN [*In an imploring voice*] Let you not take it badly, mister honey; isn't beyond the best place for you, where you'll have golden chains and shiny coats and you riding upon hunters with the ladies of the land.

[*He makes an eager sign to the Widow Quin to come to help him*]

WIDOW QUIN [*Coming over*] It's true for him, and you'd best quit off and not have that poor girl setting her mind on you, for there's Shaneen thinks she wouldn't suit you, though all is saying that she'll wed you now.

[*Christy beams with delight*]

SHAWN [*In terrified earnest*] She wouldn't suit you, and
she with the divil's own temper the way you'd be
strangling one another in a score of days. [*He makes
the movement of strangling with his hands*] It's the
like of me only that she's fit for; a quiet simple fellow
wouldn't raise a hand upon her if she scratched itself.

WIDOW QUIN [*Putting Shawn's hat on Christy*] Fit them
clothes on you anyhow, young fellow, and he'd maybe
loan them to you for the sports. [*Pushing him towards
inner door*] Fit them on and you can give your answer
when you have them tried.

CHRISTY [*Beaming, delighted with the clothes*] I will then.
I'd like herself to see me in them tweeds and hat.

[*He goes into room and shuts the door*]

SHAWN [*In great anxiety*] He'd like herself to see them.
He'll not leave us, Widow Quin. He's a score of divils
in him the way it's well-nigh certain he will wed
Pegeen.

WIDOW QUIN [*Jeeringly*] It's true all girls are fond of
courage and do hate the like of you.

SHAWN [*Walking about in desperation*] Oh, Widow
Quin, what'll I be doing now? I'd inform again him,
but he'd burst from Kilmainham and he'd be sure and
certain to destroy me. If I wasn't so God-fearing, I'd
near have courage to come behind him and run a pike
into his side. Oh, it's a hard case to be an orphan and
not to have your father that you're used to, and you'd
easy kill and make yourself a hero in the sight of all.
[*Coming up to her*] Oh, Widow Quin, will you find
me some contrivance when I've promised you a ewe?

WIDOW QUIN A ewe's a small thing, but what would you
give me if I did wed him and did save you so?

SHAWN [*With astonishment*] You?

WIDOW QUIN Aye. Would you give me the red cow you
have and the mountainy ram, and the right of way
across your rye path, and a load of dung at Michaelmas, and turbary upon the western hill?

SHAWN [*Radiant with hope*] I would, surely, and I'd give
you the wedding-ring I have, and the loan of a new
suit, the way you'd have him decent on the wedding-
day. I'd give you two kids for your dinner, and a gallon
of poteen, and I'd call the piper on the long car to your
wedding from Crossmolina or from Ballina. I'd give
you . . .

WIDOW QUIN That'll do, so, and let you whisht, for he's
coming now again.

[*Christy comes in, very natty in the new clothes.
Widow Quin goes to him admiringly*]

WIDOW QUIN If you seen yourself now, I'm thinking
you'd be too proud to speak to at all, and it'd be a pity
surely to have your like sailing from Mayo to the
western world.

CHRISTY [*As proud as a peacock*] I'm not going. If this is
a poor place itself, I'll make myself contented to be
lodging here.

[*Widow Quin makes a sign to Shawn to leave them*]

SHAWN Well, I'm going measuring the racecourse while
the tide is low, so I'll leave you the garments and my
blessing for the sports today. God bless you!

[*He wriggles out*]

WIDOW QUIN [*Admiring Christy*] Well, you're mighty
spruce, young fellow. Sit down now while you're
quiet till you talk with me.

CHRISTY [*Swaggering*] I'm going abroad on the hillside
for to seek Pegeen.

WIDOW QUIN You'll have time and plenty for to seek

Pegeen, and you heard me saying at the fall of night
the two of us should be great company.

CHRISTY From this out I'll have no want of company
when all sorts is bringing me their food and clothing
[*he swaggers to the door, tightening his belt*], the way
they'd set their eyes upon a gallant orphan cleft his
father with one blow to the breeches belt. [*He opens
door, then staggers back*] Saints of Glory! Holy angels
from the throne of light!

WIDOW QUIN [*Going over*] What ails you?

CHRISTY It's the walking spirit of my murdered da!

WIDOW QUIN [*Looking out*] Is it that tramper?

CHRISTY [*Wildly*] Where'll I hide my poor body from
that ghost of hell?

> [*The door is pushed open, and old Mahon appears on
> threshold. Christy darts in behind door*]

WIDOW QUIN [*In great amazement*] God save you, my
poor man.

MAHON [*Gruffly*] Did you see a young lad passing this
way in the early morning or the fall of night?

WIDOW QUIN You're a queer kind to walk in not saluting
at all.

MAHON Did you see the young lad?

WIDOW QUIN [*Stiffly*] What kind was he?

MAHON An ugly young streeler with a murderous gob
on him, and a little switch in his hand. I met a tramper
seen him coming this way at the fall of night.

WIDOW QUIN There's harvest hundreds do be passing these
days for the Sligo boat. For what is it you're wanting
him, my poor man?

MAHON I want to destroy him for breaking the head on
me with the clout of a loy. [*He takes off a big hat, and
shows his head in a mass of bandages and plaster, with*

79

some pride] It was he did that, and amn't I a great wonder to think I've traced him ten days with that rent in my crown?

WIDOW QUIN [*Taking his head in both hands and examining it with extreme delight*] That was a great blow. And who hit you? A robber maybe?

MAHON It was my own son hit me, and he the divil a robber, or anything else, but a dirty, stuttering lout.

WIDOW QUIN [*Letting go his skull and wiping her hands in her apron*] You'd best be wary of a mortified scalp, I think they call it, lepping around with that wound in the splendour of the sun. It was a bad blow, surely, and you should have vexed him fearful to make him strike that gash in his da.

MAHON Is it me?

WIDOW QUIN [*Amusing herself*] Aye. And isn't it a great shame when the old and hardened do torment the young?

MAHON [*Raging*] Torment him, is it? And I after holding out with the patience of a martyred saint till there's nothing but destruction on, and I'm driven out in my old age with none to aid me.

WIDOW QUIN [*Greatly amused*] It's a sacred wonder the way that wickedness will spoil a man.

MAHON My wickedness, is it? Amn't I after saying it is himself has me destroyed, and he a liar on walls, a talker of folly, a man you'd see stretched the half of the day in the brown ferns with his belly to the sun.

WIDOW QUIN Not working at all?

MAHON The divil a work, or if he did itself, you'd see him raising up a haystack like the stalk of a rush, or driving our last cow till he broke her leg at the hip, and when he wasn't at that he'd be fooling over little birds he had

—finches and felts—or making mugs at his own self in the bit of glass we had hung on the wall.

WIDOW QUIN [*Looking at Christy*] What way was he so foolish? It was running wild after the girls maybe?

MAHON [*With a shout of derision*] Running wild, is it? If he seen a red petticoat coming swinging over the hill, he'd be off to hide in the sticks, and you'd see him shooting out his sheep's eyes between the little twigs and the leaves, and his two ears rising like a hare looking out through a gap. Girls, indeed!

WIDOW QUIN It was drink maybe?

MAHON And he a poor fellow would get drunk on the smell of a pint. He'd a queer rotten stomach, I'm telling you, and when I gave him three pulls from my pipe a while since, he was taken with contortions till I had to send him in the ass-cart to the females' nurse.

WIDOW QUIN [*Clasping her hands*] Well, I never, till this day, heard tell of a man the like of that!

MAHON I'd take a mighty oath you didn't, surely, and wasn't he the laughing joke of every female woman where four baronies meet, the way the girls would stop their weeding if they seen him coming the road to let a roar at him, and call him the loony of Mahon's?

WIDOW QUIN I'd give the world and all to see the like of him. What kind was he?

MAHON A small, low fellow.

WIDOW QUIN And dark?

MAHON Dark and dirty.

WIDOW QUIN [*Considering*] I'm thinking I seen him.

MAHON [*Eagerly*] An ugly young blackguard.

WIDOW QUIN A hideous, fearful villain, and the spit of you.

MAHON Which way is he fled?

WIDOW QUIN Gone over the hills to catch a coasting
steamer to the north or south.

MAHON Could I pull up on him now?

WIDOW QUIN If you'll cross the sands below where the
tide is out, you'll be in it as soon as himself, for he had
to go round ten miles by the top of the bay. [*She
points to the door*] Strike down by the head beyond
and then follow on the roadway to the north and east.
  [*Mahon goes abruptly*]

WIDOW QUIN [*Shouting after him*] Let you give him a
good vengeance when you come up with him, but
don't put yourself in the power of the law, for it'd be a
poor thing to see a judge in his black cap reading out
his sentence on a civil warrior the like of you. [*She
swings the door to and looks at Christy, who is cower-
ing in terror, for a moment, then she bursts into a
laugh*] Well, you're the walking Playboy of the
Western World, and that's the poor man you had
divided to his breeches belt.

CHRISTY [*Looking out; then, to her*] What'll Pegeen say
when she hears that story? What'll she be saying to me
now?

WIDOW QUIN She'll knock the head of you, I'm thinking,
and drive you from the door. God help her to be taking you for a wonder, and you a little schemer making
up a story you destroyed your da.

CHRISTY [*Turning to the door, nearly speechless with
rage, half to himself*] To be letting on he was dead, and
coming back to his life, and following after me like an
old weasel tracing a rat, and coming in here laying
desolation between my own self and the fine women of
Ireland, and he a kind of carcass that you'd fling upon
the sea . . .

WIDOW QUIN [*More soberly*] There's talking for a man's one only son.

CHRISTY [*Breaking out*] His one son, is it? May I meet him with one tooth and it aching, and one eye to be seeing seven and seventy divils in the twists of the road, and one old timber leg on him to limp into the scalding grave. [*Looking out*] There he is now crossing the strands, and that the Lord God would send a high wave to wash him from the world.

WIDOW QUIN [*Scandalized*] Have you no shame? [*Putting her hand on his shoulder and turning him round*] What ails you? Near crying, is it?

CHRISTY [*In despair and grief*] Amn't I after seeing the love-light of the star of knowledge shining from her brow, and hearing words would put you thinking of the holy Brigid speaking to the infant saints, and now she'll be turning again, and speaking hard words to me, like an old woman with a spavindy ass she'd have, urging on a hill.

WIDOW QUIN There's poetry talk for a girl you'd see itching and scratching, and she with a stale stink of poteen on her from selling in the shop.

CHRISTY [*Impatiently*] It's her like is fitted to be handling merchandise in the heavens above, and what'll I be doing now, I ask you, and I a kind of wonder was jilted by the heavens when a day was by.

[*There is a distant noise of girls' voices. Widow Quin looks from window and comes to him, hurriedly*]

WIDOW QUIN You'll be doing like myself, I'm thinking, when I did destroy my man, for I'm above many's the day, odd times in great spirits, abroad in the sunshine, darning a stocking or stitching a shift; and odd times again looking out on the schooners, hookers, trawlers is sailing the sea, and I thinking on the gallant hairy fellows are drifting beyond, and myself long years living alone.

CHRISTY [*Interested*] You're like me, so.

WIDOW QUIN I am your like, and it's for that I'm taking a fancy to you, and I with my little houseen above where there'd be myself to tend you, and none to ask were you a murderer or what at all.

CHRISTY And what would I be doing if I left Pegeen?

WIDOW QUIN I've nice jobs you could be doing--gathering shells to make a whitewash for our hut within, building up a little goose-house, or stretching a new skin on an old curagh I have, and if my hut is far from all sides, it's there you'll meet the wisest old men, I tell you, at the corner of my wheel, and it's there yourself and me will have great times whispering and hugging. . . .

VOICES [*Outside, calling far away*] Christy! Christy Mahon! Christy!

CHRISTY: Is it Pegeen Mike?

WIDOW QUIN It's the young girls, I'm thinking, coming to bring you to the sports below, and what is it you'll have me to tell them now?

CHRISTY Aid me to win Pegeen. It's herself only that I'm seeking now. [*Widow Quin gets up and goes to window*] Aid me for to win her, and I'll be asking God to stretch a hand to you in the hour of death, and lead you short cuts through the Meadows of Ease, and up the floor of heaven to the Footstool of the Virgin's Son.

WIDOW QUIN There's praying!

VOICES [*Nearer*] Christy! Christy Mahon!

CHRISTY [*With agitation*] They're coming! Will you

swear to aid and save me, for the love of Christ?

WIDOW QUIN [*Looks at him for a moment*] If I aid you, will you swear to give me a right of way I want, and a mountainy ram, and a load of dung at Michaelmas, the time that you'll be master here?

CHRISTY I will, by the elements and stars of night.

WIDOW QUIN Then we'll not say a word of the old fellow, the way Pegeen won't know your story till the end of time.

CHRISTY And if he chances to return again?

WIDOW QUIN We'll swear he's a maniac, and not your da. I could take an oath I seen him raving on the sands today.

　[*Girls run in*]

SUSAN Come on to the sports below. Pegeen says you're to come.

SARA TANSEY The lepping's beginning, and we've a jockey's suit to fit upon you for the mule race on the sands below.

HONOR Come on, will you?

CHRISTY I will then if Pegeen's beyond.

SARA She's in the boreen making game of Shaneen Keogh.

CHRISTY Then I'll be going to her now.

　[*He runs out, followed by the girls*]

WIDOW QUIN Well, if the worst comes in the end of all, it'll be great game to see there's none to pity him but a widow woman, the like of me, has buried her children and destroyed her man.

　[*She goes out*]

CURTAIN

85

ACT III

Scene as before. Later in the day. Jimmy comes in, slightly drunk.

JIMMY [*Calls*] Pegeen! [*Crosses to inner door*] Pegeen Mike! [*Comes back again into the room*] Pegeen! [*Philly comes in in the same state—To Philly*] Did you see herself?

PHILLY I did not; but I sent Shawn Keogh with the ass-cart for to bear him home. [*Trying cupboards, which are locked*] Well, isn't he a nasty man to get into such staggers at a morning wake; and isn't herself the divil's daughter for locking, and she so fussy after that young gaffer, you might take your death with drouth and none to heed you?

JIMMY It's little wonder she'd be fussy, and he after bringing bankrupt ruin on the roulette man, and the trick-o'-the-loop man, and breaking the nose of the cockshot-man, and winning all in the sports below, racing, lepping, dancing, and the Lord knows what! He's right luck, I'm telling you.

PHILLY If he has, he'll be rightly hobbled yet, and he not able to say ten words without making a brag of the way he killed his father, and the great blow he hit with the loy.

JIMMY A man can't hang by his own informing, and his father should be rotten by now.

[*Old Mahon passes window slowly*]

PHILLY Supposing a man's digging spuds in that field with

a long spade, and supposing he flings up the two halves
of that skull, what'll be said then in the papers and the
courts of law?

JIMMY They'd say it was an old Dane, maybe, was
drowned in the flood. [*Old Mahon comes in and sits
down near door listening*] Did you never hear tell of
the skulls they have in the city of Dublin, ranged out
like blue jugs in a cabin of Connaught?

PHILLY And you believe that?

JIMMY [*Pugnaciously*] Didn't a lad see them and he after
coming from harvesting in the Liverpool boat? 'They
have them there,' says he, 'making a show of the great
people there was one time walking the world. White
skulls and black skulls and yellow skulls, and some with
full teeth, and some haven't only but one.'

PHILLY It was no lie, maybe, for when I was a young lad
there was a graveyard beyond the house with the remnants of a man who had thighs as long as your arm.
He was a horrid man, I'm telling you, and there was
many a fine Sunday I'd put him together for fun, and
he with shiny bones, you wouldn't meet the like of
these days in the cities of the world.

MAHON [*Getting up*] You wouldn't, is it? Lay your eyes
on that skull, and tell me where and when there was
another the like of it, is splintered only from the blow
of a loy.

PHILLY Glory be to God! And who hit you at all?

MAHON [*Triumphantly*] It was my own son hit me.
Would you believe that?

JIMMY Well, there's wonders hidden in the heart of man!

PHILLY [*Suspiciously*] And what way was it done?

MAHON [*Wandering about the room*] I'm after walking
hundreds and long scores of miles, winning clean beds

87

and the fill of my belly four times in the day, and I
doing nothing but telling stories of that naked truth.
[*He comes to them a little aggressively*] Give me a
supeen and I'll tell you now.

> [*Widow Quin comes in and stands aghast behind
> him. He is facing Jimmy and Philly, who are on
> the left*]

JIMMY Ask herself beyond. She's the stuff hidden in her
shawl.

WIDOW QUIN [*Coming to Mahon quickly*] You here, is
it? You didn't go far at all?

MAHON I seen the coasting steamer passing, and I got a
drouth upon me and a cramping leg, so I said: 'The
divil go along with him,' and turned again. [*Looking under her shawl*] And let you give me a supeen,
for I'm destroyed travelling since Tuesday was a week.

WIDOW QUIN [*Getting a glass, in a cajoling tone*] Sit
down then by the fire and take your ease for a space.
You've a right to be destroyed indeed, with your walking, and fighting, and facing the sun. [*Giving him
poteen from a stone jar she has brought in*] There now
is a drink for you, and may it be to your happiness and
length of life.

MAHON [*Taking glass greedily, and sitting down by fire*]
God increase you!

WIDOW QUIN [*Taking men to the right stealthily*] Do you
know what? That man's raving from his wound today,
for I met him a while since telling a rambling tale of
a tinker had him destroyed. Then he heard of Christy's
deed, and he up and says it was his son had cracked his
skull. Oh, isn't madness a fright, for he'll go killing
someone yet, and he thinking it's the man has struck
him so?

JIMMY [*Entirely convinced*] It's a fright surely. I knew a party was kicked in the head by a red mare, and he went killing horses a great while, till he eat the insides of a clock and died after.

PHILLY [*With suspicion*] Did he see Christy?

WIDOW QUIN He didn't. [*With a warning gesture*] Let you not be putting him in mind of him, or you'll be likely summoned if there's murder done. [*Looking round at Mahon*] Whisht! He's listening. Wait now till you hear me taking him easy and unravelling all. [*She goes to Mahon*] And what way are you feeling, mister? Are you in contentment now?

MAHON [*Slightly emotional from his drink*] I'm poorly only, for it's a hard story the way I'm left today, when it was I did tend him from his hour of birth, and he a dunce never reached his second book, the way he'd come from school, many's the day, with his legs lamed under him, and he blackened with his beatings like a tinker's ass. It's a hard story, I'm saying, the way some do have their next and nighest raising up a hand of murder on them, and some is lonesome getting their death with lamentation in the dead of night.

WIDOW QUIN [*Not knowing what to say*] To hear you talking so quiet, who'd know you were the same fellow we seen pass today?

MAHON I'm the same surely. The wrack and ruin of threescore years; and it's a terror to live that length, I tell you, and to have your sons going to the dogs against you, and you wore out scolding them, and skelping them, and God knows what.

PHILLY [*To Jimmy*] He's not raving. [*To Widow Quin*] Will you ask him what kind whas his son?

WIDOW QUIN [*To Mahon, with a peculiar look*] Was your

son that hit you a lad of one year and a score maybe, a great hand at racing and lepping and licking the world?

MAHON [*Turning on her with a roar of rage*] Didn't you hear me say he was the fool of men, the way from this out he'll know the orphan's lot, with old and young making game of him, and they swearing, raging, kicking at him like a mangy cur.

[*A great burst of cheering outside, some way off*]

MAHON [*Putting his hands to his ears*] What in the name of God do they want roaring below?

WIDOW QUIN [*With the shade of a smile*] They're cheering a young lad, the champion Playboy of the Western World.

[*More cheering*]

MAHON [*Going to window*] It'd split my heart to hear them, and I with pulses in my brain-pan for a week gone by. Is it racing they are?

JIMMY [*Looking from door*] It is, then. They are mounting him for the mule race will be run upon the sands. That's the playboy on the winkered mule.

MAHON [*Puzzled*] That lad, is it? If you said it was a fool he was, I'd have laid a mighty oath he was the likeness of my wandering son. [*Uneasily, putting his hand to his head*] Faith, I'm thinking I'll go walking for to view the race.

WIDOW QUIN [*Stopping him, sharply*] You will not. You'd best take the road to Belmullet, and not be dilly-dallying in this place where there isn't a spot you could sleep.

PHILLY [*Coming forward*] Don't mind her. Mount there on the bench and you'll have a view of the whole. They're hurrying before the tide will rise, and it'd be near over if you went down the pathway through the crags below.

MAHON [*Mounts on bench, Widow Quin beside him*] That's a right view again the edge of the sea. They're coming now from the point. He's leading. Who is he at all?

WIDOW QUIN He's the champion of the world, I tell you, and there isn't a ha'p'orth isn't falling lucky to his hands today.

PHILLY [*Looking out, interested in the race*] Look at that. They're pressing him now.

JIMMY He'll win it yet.

PHILLY Take your time, Jimmy Farrell. It's too soon to say.

WIDOW QUIN [*Shouting*] Watch him taking the gate. There's riding.

JIMMY [*Cheering*] More power to the young lad!

MAHON He's passing the third.

JIMMY He'll lick them yet.

WIDOW QUIN He'd lick them if he was running races with a score itself.

MAHON Look at the mule he has, kicking the stars.

WIDOW QUIN There was a lep! [*Catching hold of Mahon in her excitement*] He's fallen? He's mounted again! Faith, he's passing them all!

JIMMY Look at him skelping her!

PHILLY And the mountain girls hooshing him on!

JIMMY It's the last turn! The post's cleared for them now!

MAHON Look at the narrow place. He'll be into the bogs!
[*With a yell*] Good rider! He's through it again!

JIMMY He's neck and neck!

MAHON Good boy to him! Flames, but he's in!

[*Great cheering, in which all join*]

91

MAHON [*With hesitation*] What's that? They're raising him up. They're coming this way. [*With a roar of rage and astonishment*] It's Christy, by the stars of God! I'd know his way of spitting and he astride the moon.

[*He jumps down and makes a run for the door, but Widow Quin catches him and pulls him back*]

WIDOW QUIN Stay quiet, will you? That's not your son. [*To Jimmy*] Stop him, or you'll get a month for the abetting of manslaughter and be fined as well.

JIMMY I'll hold him.

MAHON [*Struggling*] Let me out! Let me out, the lot of you, till I have my vengeance on his head today.

WIDOW QUIN [*Shaking him, vehemently*] That's not your son. That's a man is going to make a marriage with the daughter of this house, a place with fine trade, with a licence, and with poteen too.

MAHON [*Amazed*] That man marrying a decent and a moneyed girl! Is it mad yous are? Is it in a crazy-house for females that I'm landed now?

WIDOW QUIN It's mad yourself is with the blow upon your head. That lad is the wonder of the western world.

MAHON I see it's my son.

WIDOW QUIN You seen that you're mad. [*Cheering outside*] Do you hear them cheering him in the zigzags of the road? Aren't you after saying that your son's a fool, and how would they be cheering a true idiot born?

MAHON [*Getting distressed*] It's maybe out of reason that that man's himself. [*Cheering again*] There's none surely will go cheering him. Oh, I'm raving with a madness that would fright the world! [*He sits down with his hand to his head*] There was one time I seen

ten scarlet divils letting on they'd cork my spirit in a
gallon can; and one time I seen rats as big as badgers
sucking the lifeblood from the butt of my lug; but
never till this day confused that dribbling idiot with
a likely man. I'm destroyed surely.

WIDOW QUIN And who'd wonder when it's your brain-
pan that is gaping now?

MAHON Then the blight of the sacred drouth upon myself
and him, for I never went mad to this day, and I not
three weeks with the Limerick girls drinking myself
silly and parlatic from the dusk to dawn. [*To Widow
Quin, suddenly*] Is my visage astray?

WIDOW QUIN It is, then. You're a sniggering maniac, a
child could see.

MAHON [*Getting up more cheerfully*] Then I'd best be
going to the union beyond, there'll be a welcome
before me, I tell you [*with great pride*], and I a terrible
and fearful case, the way that there I was one time,
screeching in a straightened waistcoat, with seven
doctors writing out my sayings in a printed book.
Would you believe that?

WIDOW QUIN If you're a wonder itself, you'd best be hasty,
for them lads caught a maniac one time and pelted the
poor creature till he ran out, raving and foaming, and
was drowned in the sea.

MAHON [*With philosophy*] It's true mankind is the divil
when your head's astray. Let me out now and I'll slip
down the boreen, and not see them so.

WIDOW QUIN [*Showing him out*] That's it. Run to the
right, and not a one will see.

[*He runs off*]

PHILLY [*Wisely*] You're at some gaming, Widow Quin;
but I'll walk after him and give him his dinner and a

time to rest, and I'll see then if he's raving or as sane
as you.

WIDOW QUIN [*Annoyed*] If you go near that lad, let you
be wary of your head, I'm saying. Didn't you hear
him telling he was crazed at times?

PHILLY I heard him telling a power; and I'm thinking
we'll have right sport before night will fall.

[*He goes out*]

JIMMY Well, Philly's a conceited and foolish man. How
could that madman have his senses and his brain-pan
slit? I'll go after them and see him turn on Philly now.

[*He goes; Widow Quin hides poteen behind counter.
Then hubbub outside*]

VOICES There you are! Good jumper! Grand lepper!
Darlint boy! He's the racer! Bear him on, will you!

[*Christy comes in, in jockey's dress, with Pegeen
Mike, Sara, and other girls and men*]

PEGEEN [*To crowd*] Go on now, and don't destroy him,
and he drenching with sweat. Go along, I'm saying,
and have your tug-of-warring till he's dried his
skin.

CROWD Here's his prizes! A bagpipes! A fiddle was played
by a poet in the years gone by! A flat and three-
thorned blackthorn would lick the scholars out of
Dublin town!

CHRISTY [*Taking prizes from the men*] Thank you kindly,
the lot of you. But you'd say it was little only I did this
day if you'd seen me a while since striking my one
single blow.

TOWN CRIER [*Outside ringing a bell*] Take notice, last
event of this day! Tug-of-warring on the green
below! Come on, the lot of you! Great achievements
for all Mayo men!

94

PEGEEN Go on and leave him for to rest and dry. Go on, I tell you, for he'll do no more.

[*She hustles crowd out; Widow Quin following them*]

MEN [*Going*] Come on, then. Good luck for the while!

PEGEEN [*Radiantly, wiping his face with her shawl*] Well, you're the lad, and you'll have great times from this out when you could win that wealth of prizes, and you sweating in the heat of noon!

CHRISTY [*Looking at her with delight*] I'll have great times if I win the crowning prize I'm seeking now, and that's your promise that you'll wed me in a fortnight, when our banns is called.

PEGEEN [*Backing away from him*] You've right daring to go ask me that, when all knows you'll be starting to some girl in your own townland, when your father's rotten in four months, or five.

CHRISTY [*Indignantly*] Starting from you, is it? [*He follows her*] I will not, then, and when the airs is warming, in four months or five, it's then yourself and me should be pacing Neifin in the dews of night, the times sweet smells do be rising, and you'd see a little, shiny new moon, maybe sinking on the hills.

PEGEEN [*Looking at him playfully*] And it's that kind of a poacher's love you'd make, Christy Mahon, on the sides of Neifin, when the night is down?

CHRISTY It's little you'll think if my love's a poacher's, or an earl's itself, when you'll feel my two hands stretched around you, and I squeezing kisses on your puckered lips, till I'd feel a kind of pity for the Lord God is all ages sitting lonesome in His golden chair.

PEGEEN That'll be right fun, Christy Mahon, and any girl

would walk her heart out before she'd meet a young man was your like for eloquence, or talk at all.

CHRISTY [*Encouraged*] Let you wait, to hear me talking, till we're astray in Erris, when Good Friday's by, drinking a sup from a well, and making mighty kisses with our wetted mouths, or gaming in a gap of sunshine, with yourself stretched back unto your necklace, in the flowers of the earth.

PEGEEN [*In a low voice, moved by his tone*] I'd be nice so, is it?

CHRISTY [*With rapture*] If the mitred bishops seen you that time, they'd be the like of the holy prophets, I'm thinking, do be straining the bars of paradise to lay eyes on the Lady Helen of Troy, and she abroad, pacing back and forward, with a nosegay in her golden shawl.

PEGEEN [*With real tenderness*] And what is it I have, Christy Mahon, to make me fitting entertainment for the like of you, that has such poet's talking, and such bravery of heart?

CHRISTY [*In a low voice*] Isn't there the light of seven heavens in your heart alone, the way you'll be an angel's lamp to me from this out, and I abroad in the darkness, spearing salmons in the Owen or the Carrowmore?

PEGEEN If I was your wife I'd be along with you those nights, Christy Mahon, the way you'd see I was a great hand at coaxing bailiffs, or coining funny nicknames for the stars of night.

CHRISTY You, is it? Taking your death in the hailstones, or in the fogs of dawn.

PEGEEN Yourself and me would shelter easy in a narrow bush [*with a qualm of dread*]; but we're only talking, maybe, for this would be a poor, thatched place to hold a fine lad is the like of you.

CHRISTY [*Putting his arm round her*] If I wasn't a good Christian, it's on my naked knees I'd be saying my prayers and paters to every jackstraw you have roofing your head, and every stony pebble is paving the lane-way to your door.

PEGEEN [*Radiantly*] If that's the truth I'll be burning candles from this out to the miracles of God that have brought you from the south today, and I with my gowns bought ready, the way that I can wed you, and not wait at all.

CHRISTY It's miracles, and that's the truth. Me there toiling a long while, and walking a long while, not knowing at all I was drawing all times nearer to this holy day.

PEGEEN And myself, a girl, was tempted often to go sailing the seas till I'd marry a Jew-man, with ten kegs of gold, and I not knowing at all there was the like of you drawing nearer, like the stars of God.

CHRISTY And to think I'm long years hearing women talking that talk, to all bloody fools, and this the first time I've heard the like of your voice talking sweetly for my own delight.

PEGEEN And to think it's me is talking sweetly, Christy Mahon, and I the fright of seven townlands for my biting tongue. Well, the heart's a wonder; and, I'm thinking, there won't be our like in Mayo, for gallant lovers, from this hour today. [*Drunken singing is heard outside*] There's my father coming from the wake, and when he's had his sleep we'll tell him, for he's peaceful then.

[*They separate*]

97

MICHAEL [*Singing outside*]

> The jailer and the turnkey
> They quickly ran us down,
> And brought us back as prisoners
> Once more to Cavan town

[*He comes in supported by Shawn*]

> There we lay bewailing
> All in a prison bound . . .

[*He sees Christy. Goes and shakes him drunkenly by the hand, while Pegeen and Shawn talk on the left*]

MICHAEL [*To Christy*] The blessing of God and the holy angels on your head, young fellow. I hear tell you're after winning all in the sports below; and wasn't it a shame I didn't bear you along with me to Kate Cassidy's wake, a fine, stout lad, the like of you, for you'd never see the match of it for flows of drink, the way when we sunk her bones at noonday in her narrow grave, there were five men, aye, and six men, stretched out retching speechless on the holy stones.

CHRISTY [*Uneasily, watching Pegeen*] Is that the truth?

MICHAEL It is, then; and aren't you a louty schemer to go burying your poor father unbeknownst when you'd a right to throw him on the crupper of a Kerry mule and drive him westwards, like holy Joseph in the days gone by, the way we could have given him a decent burial, and not have him rotting beyond, and not a Christian drinking a smart drop to the glory of his soul?

CHRISTY [*Gruffly*] It's well enough he's lying, for the likes of him.

MICHAEL [*Slapping him on the back*] Well, aren't you a hardened slayer? It'll be a poor thing for the house-

98

hold man where you go sniffing for a female wife; and [*pointing to Shawn*] look beyond at that shy and decent Christian I have chosen for my daughter's hand, and I after getting the gilded dispensation this day for to wed them now.

CHRISTY And you'll be wedding them this day, is it?

MICHAEL [*Drawing himself up*] Aye. Are you thinking, if I'm drunk itself. I'd leave my daughter living single with a little frisky rascal is the like of you?

PEGEEN [*Breaking away from Shawn*] Is it the truth the dispensation's come?

MICHAEL [*Triumphantly*] Father Reilly's after reading it in gallous Latin, and 'It's come in the nick of time,' says he; 'so I'll wed them in a hurry, dreading that young gaffer who'd capsize the stars.'

PEGEEN [*Fiercely*] He's missed his nick of time, for it's that lad, Christy Mahon, that I'm wedding now.

MICHAEL [*Loudly, with horror*] You'd be making him a son to me, and he wet and crusted with his father's blood?

PEGEEN Aye. Wouldn't it be a bitter thing for a girl to go marrying the like of Shaneen, and he a middling kind of a scarecrow, with no savagery or fine words in him at all?

MICHAEL [*Gasping and sinking on a chair*] Oh, aren't you a heathen daughter to go shaking the fat of my heart, and I swamped and drowned with the weight of drink? Would you have them turning on me the way that I'd be roaring to the dawn of day with the wind upon my heart? Have you not a word to aid me, Shaneen? Are you not jealous at all?

SHAWN [*In great misery*] I'd be afeard to be jealous of a man did slay his da.

PEGEEN Well, it'd be a poor thing to go marrying your like. I'm seeing there's a world of peril for an orphan girl, and isn't it a great blessing I didn't wed you before himself came walking from the west or south?

SHAWN It's a queer story you'd go picking a dirty tramp up from the highways of the world.

PEGEEN [*Playfully*] And you think you're a likely beau to go straying along with the shiny Sundays of the opening year, when it's sooner on a bullock's liver you'd put a poor girl thinking than on the lily or the rose?

SHAWN And have you no mind of my weight of passion, and the holy dispensation, and the drift of heifers I'm giving, and the golden ring?

PEGEEN I'm thinking you're too fine for the like of me, Shawn Keogh of Killakeen, and let you go off till you'd find a radiant lady with droves of bullocks on the plains of Meath, and herself bedizened in the diamond jewelleries of Pharaoh's ma. That'd be your match, Shaneen. So God save you now!

[*She retreats behind Christy*]

SHAWN Won't you hear me telling you . . . ?

CHRISTY [*With ferocity*] Take yourself from this, young fellow, or I'll maybe add a murder to my deeds today.

MICHAEL [*Springing up with a shriek*] Murder is it? Is it mad yous are? Would you go making murder in this place, and it piled with poteen for our drink tonight? Go on to the foreshore if it's fighting you want, where the rising tide will wash all traces from the memory of man.

[*Pushing Shawn towards Christy*]

SHAWN [*Shaking himself free, and getting behind*

Michael] I'll not fight him, Michael James. I'd liefer
live a bachelor, simmering in passions to the end of
time, than face a lepping savage the like of him has
descended from the Lord knows where. Strike him
yourself, Michael James, or you'll lose my drift of
heifers and my blue bull from Sneem.

MICHAEL Is it me fight him, when it's father-slaying he's
bred to now? [*Pushing Shawn*] Go on, you fool, and
fight him now.

SHAWN [*Coming forward a little*] Will I strike him with
my hand?

MICHAEL Take the loy is on your western side.

SHAWN I'd be afeard of the gallows if I struck with
that.

CHRISTY [*Taking up the loy*] Then I'll make you face
the gallows or quit off from this.

[*Shawn flies out of the door*]

CHRISTY Well, fine weather be after him [*going to
Michael, coaxingly*], and I'm thinking you wouldn't
wish to have that quaking blackguard in your house
at all. Let you give us your blessing and hear her swear
her faith to me, for I'm mounted on the spring-tide
of the stars of luck, the way it'll be good for any to
have me in the house.

PEGEEN [*At the other side of Michael*] Bless us now, for
I swear to God I'll wed him, and I'll not renege.

MICHAEL [*Standing up in the centre, holding on to both
of them*] It's the will of God, I'm thinking, that all
should win an easy or a cruel end, and it's the will
of God that all should rear up lengthy families for
the nurture of the earth. What's a single man, I ask
you, eating a bit in one house and drinking a sup in
another, and he with no place of his own, like an

old braying jackass strayed upon the rocks? [*To Christy*] It's many would be in dread to bring your like into their house for to end them, maybe, with a sudden end; but I'm a decent man of Ireland, and I liefer face the grave untimely and I seeing a score of grandsons growing up little gallant swearers by the name of God, than go peopling my bedside with puny weeds the like of what you'd breed, I'm thinking, out of Shaneen Keogh. [*He joins their hands*] A daring fellow is the jewel of the world, and a man did split his father's middle with a single clout should have the bravery of ten, so may God and Mary and St. Patrick bless you, and increase you from this mortal day.

CHRISTY *and* PEGEEN Amen, O Lord!

> [*Hubbub outside. Old Mahon rushes in, followed by all the crowd, and Widow Quin. He makes a rush at Christy, knocks him down, and begins to beat him*]

PEGEEN [*Dragging back his arm*] Stop that, will you? Who are you at all?

MAHON His father, God forgive me!

PEGEEN [*Drawing back*] Is it rose from the dead?

MAHON Do you think I look so easy quenched with the tap of a loy?

> [*Beats Christy again*]

PEGEEN [*Glaring at Christy*] And it's lies you told, letting on you had him slitted, and you nothing at all.

CHRISTY [*Catching Mahon's stick*] He's not my father. He's a raving maniac would scare the world. [*Pointing to Widow Quin*] Herself knows it is true.

CROWD You're fooling, Pegeen! The Widow Quin seen him this day, and you likely knew! You're a liar!

CHRISTY [*Dumbfounded*] It's himself was a liar, lying stretched out with an open head on him, letting on he was dead.

MAHON Weren't you off racing the hills before I got my breath with the start I had seeing you turn on me at all?

PEGEEN And to think of the coaxing glory we had given him, and he after doing nothing but hitting a soft blow and chasing northward in a sweat of fear. Quit off from this.

CHRISTY [*Piteously*] You've seen my doings this day, and let you save me from the old man; for why would you be in such a scorch of haste to spur me to destruction now?

PEGEEN It's there your treachery is spurring me, till I'm hard set to think you're the one I'm after lacing in my heart-strings half an hour gone by. [*To Mahon*] Take him on from this, for I think bad the world should see me raging for a Munster liar, and the fool of men.

MAHON Rise up now to retribution, and come on with me.

CROWD [*Jeeringly*] There's the playboy! There's the lad thought he'd rule the roost in Mayo! Slate him now, mister.

CHRISTY [*Getting up in shy terror*] What is it drives you to torment me here, when I'd asked the thunders of the might of God to blast me if I ever did hurt to any saving only that one single blow.

MAHON [*Loudly*] If you didn't, you're a poor good-for-nothing, and isn't it by the like of you the sins of the whole world are committed?

CHRISTY [*Raising his hands*] In the name of the Almighty God . . .

MAHON Leave troubling the Lord God. Would you have
Him sending down droughts, and fevers, and the old
hen and the cholera morbus?

CHRISTY [*To Widow Quin*] Will you come between us
and protect me now?

WIDOW QUIN I've tried a lot, God help me, and my share
is done.

CHRISTY [*Looking round in desperation*] And I must go
back into my torment is it, or run off like a vagabond
straying through the unions with the dust of August
making mudstains in the gullet of my throat; or the
winds of March blowing on me till I'd take an oath
I felt them making whistles of my ribs within?

SARA Ask Pegeen to aid you. Her like does often change.

CHRISTY I will not, then, for there's torment in the
splendour of her like, and she a girl any moon of
midnight would take pride to meet, facing southwards
on the heaths of Keel. But what did I want crawling
forward to scorch my understanding at her flaming
brow?

PEGEEN [*To Mahon, vehemently, fearing she will break
into tears*] Take him on from this or I'll set the young
lads to destroy him here.

MAHON [*Going to him, shaking his stick*] Come on now if
you wouldn't have the company to see you skelped.

PEGEEN [*Half laughing, through her tears*] That's it, now
the world will see him pandied, and he an ugly liar was
playing off the hero, and the fright of men.

CHRISTY [*To Mahon, very sharply*] Leave me go!

CROWD That's it. Now, Christy. If them two set fighting,
it will lick the world.

MAHON [*Making a grab at Christy*] Come here to me.

CHRISTY [*More threateningly*] Leave me go, I'm saying.

MAHON I will, maybe, when your legs is limping, and your back is blue.

CROWD Keep it up, the two of you. I'll back the old one. Now the playboy.

CHRISTY [*In low and intense voice*] Shut your yelling, for if you're after making a mighty man of me this day by the power of a lie, you're setting me now to think if it's a poor thing to be lonesome it's worse, maybe, go mixing with the fools of earth.

[*Mahon makes a movement towards him*]

CHRISTY [*Almost shouting*] Keep off . . . lest I do show a blow unto the lot of you would set the guardian angels winking in the clouds above.

[*He swings round with a sudden rapid movement and picks up a loy*]

CROWD [*Half frightened, half amused*] He's going mad! Mind yourselves! Run from the idiot!

CHRISTY If I am an idiot, I'm after hearing my voice this day saying words would raise the top-knot on a poet in a merchant's town. I've won your racing, and your lepping, and . . .

MAHON Shut your gullet and come on with me.

CHRISTY I'm going, but I'll stretch you first.

[*He runs at old Mahon with the loy, chases him out of the door, followed by crowd and Widow Quin. There is a great noise outside, then a yell, and dead silence for a moment. Christy comes in, half dazed, and goes to fire*]

WIDOW QUIN [*Coming in hurriedly, and going to him*] They're turning again you. Come on, or you'll be hanged, indeed.

CHRISTY I'm thinking from this out, Pegeen'll be giving me praises, the same as in the hours gone by.

WIDOW QUIN [*Impatiently*] Come by the back door. I'd think bad to have you stifled on the gallows tree.

CHRISTY [*Indignantly*] I will not, then. What good'd be my lifetime if I left Pegeen?

WIDOW QUIN Come on, and you'll be no worse than you were last night; and you with a double murder this time to be telling to the girls.

CHRISTY I'll not leave Pegeen Mike.

WIDOW QUIN [*Impatiently*] Isn't there the match of her in every parish public, from Binghamstown unto the plain of Meath? Come on, I tell you, and I'll find you finer sweethearts at each waning moon.

CHRISTY It's Pegeen I'm seeking only, and what'd I care if you brought me a drift of chosen females, standing in their shifts itself, maybe, from this place to the eastern world?

SARA [*Runs in, pulling off one of her petticoats*] They're going to hang him. [*Holding out petticoat and shawl*] Fit these upon him, and let him run off to the east.

WIDOW QUIN He's raving now; but we'll fit them on him, and I'll take him in the ferry to the Achill boat.

CHRISTY [*Struggling feebly*] Leave me go, will you? when I'm thinking of my luck today, for she will wed me surely, and I a proven hero in the end of all.

[*They try to fasten petticoat round him*]

WIDOW QUIN Take his left hand and we'll pull him now. Come on, young fellow.

CHRISTY [*Suddenly starting up*] You'll be taking me from her? You're jealous, is it, of her wedding me? Go on from this.

[*He snatches up a stool, and threatens them with it*]

WIDOW QUIN [*Going*] It's in the madhouse they should

put him, not in jail, at all. We'll go by the back door to call the doctor, and we'll save him so.

[*She goes out, with Sara, through inner room. Men crowd in the doorway. Christy sits down again by the fire*]

MICHAEL [*In a terrified whisper*] Is the old lad killed surely?

PHILLY I'm after feeling the last gasps quitting his heart.
[*They peer in at Christy*]

MICHAEL [*With a rope*] Look at the way he is. Twist a hangman's knot on it, and slip it over his head, while he's not minding at all.

PHILLY Let you take it, Shaneen. You're the soberest of all that's here.

SHAWN Is it me to go near him, and he the wickedest and worst with me? Let you take it, Pegeen Mike.

PEGEEN Come on, so.

[*She goes forward with the others, and they drop the double hitch over his head*]

CHRISTY What ails you?

SHAWN [*Triumphantly, as they pull the rope tight on his arms*] Come on to the peelers, till they stretch you now.

CHRISTY Me!

MICHAEL If we took pity on you the Lord God would, maybe, bring us ruin from the law today, so you'd best come easy, for hanging is an easy and a speedy end.

CHRISTY I'll not stir. [*To Pegeen*] And what is it you'll say to me, and I after doing it this time in the face of all?

PEGEEN I'll say, a strange man is a marvel, with his mighty talk; but what's a squabble in your back yard, and the blow of a loy, have taught me that there's a great gap

107

between a gallous story and a dirty deed. [*To men*]
Take him on from this, or the lot of us will be likely
put on trial for his deed today.

CHRISTY [*With horror in his voice*] And it's yourself will
send me off, to have a horny-fingered hangman hitch-
ing slip-knots at the butt of my ear.

MEN [*Pulling rope*] Come on, will you?
  [*He is pulled down on the floor*]

CHRISTY [*Twisting his legs round the table*] Cut the rope,
Pegeen, and I'll quit the lot of you, and live from this
out, like the madman of Keel, eating muck and green
weeds on the faces of the cliffs.

PEGEEN And leave us to hang, is it, for a saucy liar,
the like of you? [*To men*] Take him on, out
from this.

SHAWN Pull a twist on his neck, and squeeze him so.

PHILLY Twist yourself. Sure he cannot hurt you, if you
keep your distance from his teeth alone.

SHAWN I'm afeard of him. [*To Pegeen*] Lift a lighted
sod, will you, and scorch his leg.

PEGEEN [*Blowing the fire with a bellows*] Leave go now,
young fellow, or I'll scorch your shins.

CHRISTY You're blowing for to torture me. [*His voice
rising and growing stronger*] That's your kind, is it?
Then let the lot of you be wary, for, if I've to face the
gallows, I'll have a gay march down, I tell you, and
shed the blood of some of you before I die.

SHAWN [*In terror*] Keep a good hold, Philly. Be wary,
for the love of God. For I'm thinking he would liefest
wreak his pains on me.

CHRISTY [*Almost gaily*] If I do lay my hands on you, it's
the way you'll be at the fall of night, hanging as a
scarecrow for the fowls of hell. Ah, you'll have a

gallous jaunt, I'm saying, coaching out through limbo
with my father's ghost.

SHAWN [*To Pegeen*] Make haste, will you? Oh, isn't he a
holy terror, and isn't it true for Father Reilly, that all
drink's a curse that has the lot of you so shaky and
uncertain now?

CHRISTY If I can wring a neck among you, I'll have a royal
judgment looking on the trembling jury in the courts
of law. And won't there be crying out in Mayo the day
I'm stretched upon the rope, with ladies in their silks
and satins snivelling in their lacy kerchiefs, and they
rhyming songs and ballads on the terror of my fate?

[*He squirms round on the floor and bites Shawn's
leg*]

SHAWN [*Shrieking*] My leg's bit on me. He's the like of
a mad dog, I'm thinking, the way that I will surely
die.

CHRISTY [*Delighted with himself*] You will, then, the way
you can shake out hell's flags of welcome for my coming in two weeks or three, for I'm thinking Satan hasn't
many have killed their da in Kerry, and in Mayo too.

[*Old Mahon comes in behind on all fours and looks
on unnoticed*]

MEN [*To Pegeen*] Bring the sod, will you?

PEGEEN [*Coming over*] God help him so.

[*Burns his leg*]

CHRISTY [*Kicking and screaming*] Oh, glory be to God!

[*He kicks loose from the table, and they all drag him
towards the door*]

JIMMY [*Seeing old Mahon*] Will you look what's come
in?

[*They all drop Christy and run left*]

CHRISTY [*Scrambling on his knees face to face with old

Mahon] Are you coming to be killed a third time, or what ails you now?

MAHON For what is it they have you tied?

CHRISTY They're taking me to the peelers to have me hanged for slaying you.

MICHAEL [*Apologetically*] It is the will of God that all should guard their little cabins from the treachery of law, and what would my daughter be doing if I was ruined or was hanged itself?

MAHON [*Grimly, loosening Christy*] It's little I care if you put a bag on her back, and went picking cockles till the hour of death; but my son and myself will be going our own way, and we'll have great times from this out telling stories of the villainy of Mayo, and the fools is here. [*To Christy, who is freed*] Come on now.

CHRISTY Go with you, is it? I will then, like a gallant captain with his heathen slave. Go on now and I'll see you from this day stewing my oatmeal and washing my spuds, for I'm master of all fights from now. [*Pushing Mahon*] Go on, I'm saying.

MAHON Is it me?

CHRISTY Not a word out of you. Go on from this.

MAHON [*Walking out and looking back at Christy over his shoulder*] Glory be to God! [*With a broad smile*] I am crazy again.

[*Goes*]

CHRISTY Ten thousand blessings upon all that's here, for you've turned me a likely gaffer in the end of all, the way I'll go romancing through a romping lifetime from this hour to the dawning of the Judgment Day.

[*He goes out*]

MICHAEL By the will of God, we'll have peace now for our drinks. Will you draw the porter, Pegeen?

SHAWN [*Going up to her*] It's a miracle Father Reilly can wed us in the end of all, and we'll have none to trouble us when his vicious bite is healed.

PEGEEN [*Hitting him a box on the ear*] Quit my sight. [*Putting her shawl over her head and breaking out into wild lamentations*] Oh, my grief, I've lost him surely. I've lost the only Playboy of the Western World.

CURTAIN

Notes

(These notes are intended to serve the needs of overseas students as well as those of English-born users.)

Title

    Playboy — various interpretations — a dare-devil, a player of games, a trifler who takes nothing seriously, an actor — all of which Christy exemplifies at some point.

    the Western World — traditionally a mythical land located to the west of Ireland but is used in the play to mean both the western coast of Ireland and the land beyond i.e. America.

38 *a squatter* — countless squatters had settled in huts throughout N.W. Ireland without any real likelihood of being able to maintain themselves. They would sow patches of potatoes in early spring and trust to good luck and their skill in begging to keep themselves and their families.

38 *Pegeen Mike* — Peg is a common nickname for Margaret; -een means little. 'Mike' shows she is Michael Flaherty's daughter.

38 *her cousin* — Widow Quin's name was restored to the List of Persons at a late stage of the printing process, having been accidentally omitted from Synge's final typescript. By placing her name before that of Shawn Keogh, the printer thus obscured Pegeen's blood relationship with Shawn by making the Widow and Shawn cousins by mistake. It is Pegeen and Shawn that are cousins.

38 *A Bellman* — Town Crier.

38 *Mayo* — Wild, infertile county on N.W. seaboard of Ireland.

38 The name of Nelly McLaughlin, the fourth village girl, was omitted from the List of Persons — probably because her part was cut and her lines given to Honor Blake in the first production.

41 *shebeen* — low wayside public house — here without the usual connotation of a place serving spirits illegally.

41 *the usual peasant dress* — described by Synge as 'a short red petticoat over bare feet and legs, a faded uncertain bodice and a white or blue rag swathing the head'.

41 *porter* — dark brown, rather bitter beer.

41 *creel cart* — cart with temporary wicker sides and back.

41 *Where's himself?* — Where's the man of the house?

42 *wake* — a watch beside the dead, accompanied by feasting and drinking.

42 *the scruff of the hill* — the slope below the summit of the hill.

42 *dispensation* — a licence granted by a pope, archbishop or bishop to allow a person to do what is forbidden by ecclesiastical law. Shawn and Pegeen need permission to marry since they are cousins.

43 *peeler* — a policeman — from the name of Sir Robert Peel who founded the Royal Irish Constabulary.

43 *maiming ewes* — a favourite method of paying off grudges against neighbours and landlords.

43 *a great warrant to tell* — highly skilled and famous for telling.

43 *conceit* — desire.

44 *feeling a kind of fellow* — feeling that there is a kind of fellow.

44 *furzy* — overgrown with gorse.

44 *don't let on* — don't say anthing about.

44 *great blabbing* — great deal of gossipping.

44 *whisht* — be quiet.

45 *quitting off* — going away, clearing off.

45 *Stooks of the Dead Women* — rocks on the sea shore, pointed like 'stooks' — conical clusters of sheaves of oats set up to dry. They are actual rocks in West Kerry.

45 *with a drop taken* — having drunk rather a lot of alcohol.

45 *piling the turf* — piling up the slabs of peat to be used as fuel on the fire. Peat is decomposed vegetable matter partly carbonised by chemical change which forms into areas of land called bogs.

45 *tinkers* — menders of pots, pans etc. who travelled about and were regarded as thieves.

45 *militia* — part-time soldiers who had a reputation for brutality and licentiousness.

45 *bad cess* — bad luck — 'cess' is probably an abbreviation of 'success'.

46 *in the grip of the ditch* — in the hollow under the bank.

47 *a penny pot-boy* — a serving man in a cheap public house.

48 *woman of the house* — lady in charge of the establishment.

48 *polis* — police, pronounced pólis.

48 *bona fide* — a person living more than three miles away and therefore entitled under the then licensing hours to obtain a drink as a traveller outside normal hours.

48 *You're wanting* — 'wanted' i.e. by the police for some crime but also probably punning on the conventional meaning, 'needy'.

48 *broken harvest* – poor potato harvest, interrupted by bad weather.

48 *the ended wars* – the Boer War fought in South Africa in 1881 and 1899–1902. Irish labourers fought on the side of the Dutch settlers against the English.

49 *strong* – of substance, having a farm which gives a good living.

49 *from the butt of his tail pocket* – from the bottom of the pocket of a swallow-tailed coat, part of the formal dress of the older men.

49 *bailiffs* – officers of the law who took possession of land or houses in case of debt.

49 *The divil a one* – not a single one.

49 *agents* – similar to bailiffs but employed by landowners.

50 *Munster* – along with Ulster, Leinster and Connacht, one of the four provinces of Ireland.

50 *Puzzle-the-world* – a total enigma.

50 *Luthers of the preaching north* – Protestants so-called after Martin Luther, founder of German Protestantism. From early 17th century English and Scottish Protestants had tended to settle in the north rather than the south.

50 *Kruger* – Paul Kruger (1825–1904), President of Transvaal Republic, one of the leaders of the Boers.

51 *Tuesday was a week* – a week last Tuesday.

51 *mister honey* – my dear man.

51 *crusty* – short tempered.

51 *I've no licence* – i.e. gun licence – necessary if in possession of a firearm.

51 *I'm told, in the big world, it's bloody knives they use* – a reference to the Phoenix Park murders of 1882 in which the Chief Secretary for Ireland, Lord Frederick Cavendish, and his Under-Secretary were killed by nationalists armed with surgical knives.

51 *hanged his dog from the licence* – hanged his dog to save paying the licence.

52 *riz the loy* – raised the loy –spade-like implement with long thin blade.

52 *spuds* – potatoes.

52 *sense of Solomon* – Solomon was a king of Israel renowned for his wisdom.

52 *poteen* – whiskey illegally distilled, usually from potatoes.

53 *pitchpike* – two-pronged fork used for hay.

53 *loosed khaki cut-throats* – soldiers returned from the Boer War.

53 *drouthy* — thirsty.

54 *humbugging* — fooling, cheating.

54 *and let him put you in the holy brotherhoods* — let him turn you into a monk i.e. holy and celibate.

55 *a quality name* — an aristocratic name.

56 *cot* — cottage.

56 *scribes of bog* — strips of wet peat land.

56 *streeleen* — gossip.

56 *Owen Roe O'Sullivan* — best-known of all the Munster poets, a sort of Irish Robert Burns.

56 *Dingle Bay* — is in Kerry.

56 *a power of rings* — a great many rings.

57 *the eastern world* — traditionally a mythical land located to the east of Ireland but used here to mean both the eastern coast of Ireland (richer and more fertile) and the land beyond i.e. Europe and the East.

58 *St. Martin's Day* — 11 November.

58 *like a gaudy officer* — reference to the brilliant colours in the dress of officers at the time.

58 *shying clods* — throwing lumps of earth.

58 *banbhs* — piglets, pronounced 'boniffs'.

59 *stringing gabble* — chattering away.

59 *your curiosity man* — human prodigy.

60 *I've their word* — I have their orders.

60 *priesteen* — little priest, used here contemptuously.

60 *da* — father.

60 *walk on from this* — walk away from here, ignoring this matter.

60 *penny poets* — ballad writers selling their verses at fairs.

60 *himself* — her husband.

60 *overed* — recovered from.

61 *let you a wink* — give you as much as a wink — traditional sign of flirtation.

61 *houseen* — little house.

61 *a perch off* — a perch is a rod of definite length for measuring land, usually 5½ yards but here used to suggest a very short distance.

62 *felt the elements of a Christian* — detected the parts of a human being.

62 *a sop of grass tobacco* — a small amount of dried but uncured tobacco leaf.

62 *rating* — scolding.

62 *liefer* — rather.

62 *it's a terror to be aged a score* — score = 20, i.e. Pegeen is showing the ferocity of youth.

62 *a sheepskin parchment* — the dispensation referred to in note p.42.

64 *to drunken* — to have drunk.

65 *making game of* — making fun of.

66 *cnuceen* — little hill.

67 *a little cut* — slice.

67 *pitching* — throwing.

67 *in place of nursing a feast* — instead of hoarding the items for a feast.

67 *Are you fasting or fed?* — Are you hungry or have you eaten?

67 *you're the lot* — you're the limit.

68 *gamy* — merry.

69 *dray* — low cart without sides for carrying heavy loads.

69 *lep* — leap.

70 *supeen* — little sip.

70 *jobbing jockies* — free-lance horse-tamers who travel the country ready to break in a horse and occasionally ride in a race.

70 — *juries fill their stomachs selling judgments of the English law* — jury members who accept bribes by giving the verdict desired by the English who ruled Ireland at the time.

70 *white shift or shirt* — a shift is a woman's undergarment like a slip, worn next to the skin and reaching to the knees. For a woman to possess a white shift and a man a white shirt was considered a basic requirement for respectability.

70 *the dying of the flood* — as long as can be remembered — a reference to The Flood survived only by Noah and his family in the Bible; hence, the beginning of recorded time.

71 *lepping the stones* — crossing by stepping stones.

71 *three perches* — not very far away — see note p.61.

72 *quick-lime* — used to aid rapid deterioration of dead bodies.

72 *frish-frash* — a thin gruel made of such things as coarse grain, shredded cabbage with a beaten egg.

72 *shut of jeopardy* — free from danger.

73 *Esau* — in the Old Testament sold his birthright to Jacob for a 'mess of red pottage'.

73 *Cain and Abel* — Cain killed his brother Abel in the first murder recorded in the Bible.

73 *Neifin* — a mountain in Mayo.

73 *Erris plain* — district in the north-west of Mayo.

73 *circuit judges* — judges of the High Court who periodically visit principal towns to try the more serious cases.

74 *hard set* — having great difficulty.

74 *letting on* — pretending.

74 *stretching out the earth between us* — putting a great distance between us.

74 *wattle* — stick.

74 *mitch off* — truant.

75 *thraneen* — a little stalk of withered grass i.e. something worthless.

74 *cleeve* — basket.

74 *your mountainy sheep eating cabbages* — if sheep get among any green vegetable, they eat their way greedily into the crop which rapidly swells in their stomachs causing great pain and sometimes death.

77 *Kilmainham* — notorious gaol in Dublin.

77 *a pike* — a pitchfork.

78 *rye path* — path by the side of a patch of rye.

78 *Michaelmas* — 29 September.

78 *turbary* — the right to cut turf (peat) for fuel from a stretch of bog.

78 *long car* — type of wagon used for postal deliveries etc. at this time.

79 *not saluting at all* — giving no form of greeting to those present - this would be regarded as the height of rudeness.

79 *streeler* — ragged youth, slovenly person.

79 *gob* — mouth.

79 *switch* — stick.

79 *Sligo* — a busy port to the west of County Mayo. 'Harvest hundreds' would embark there on the way to temporary employment in Scotland or England.

80 *a liar on walls* — one who leans lazily against walls chatting, perhaps lying, to his friends. Editors are divided as to whether this should read 'liar' or 'lier'. A pun is presumably intended.

80 *The divil a work* — no work at all.

81 *felts* — thrushes.

81 *making mugs* — making faces.

81 *the spit of you* — the spitting image or exact likeness of you.

82 *an old weasel tracing a rat* — a weasel works from side to side picking up the scent of its prey.

82 *a kind of carcass that you'd fling upon the sea* — dead sheep. and cattle would not be buried but pushed over the cliff into the Atlantic.

83 *the star of knowledge* — idea taken from Irish poetry. Refers to love opening up new dimensions of experience or a star that guides us.

83 *spavindy ass* — a donkey lame with spavin, a disease of the hock-joint.

83 *hookers* — heavily built sailing cutters used for carrying cargo to the islands.

84 *curragh* — light boat made of wicker work covered with hide or canvas. Pronounced 'curra'.

84 *at the corner of my wheel* — old men come in to gossip while she is working at her spinning wheel.

84 *Meadows of Ease* — Paradise.

84 *the Footstool of the Virgin's Son* — stool in Heaven on which Christ's feet rest.

85 *boreen* — lane.

86 *to get into such staggers* — so drunk that he is staggering about.

86 *gaffer* — master.

86 *drouth* — thirst.

86 *trick o' the loop man* — man in charge of hoop-la, a game where small hoops have to be thrown over objects.

86 *cockshot man* — man in a sideshow who let people pay to throw sticks at him.

86 *hobbled* — impeded, i.e. caught and arrested.

89 *easy* — quietly.

90 *a mangy cur* — a scruffy dog whose coat is diseased.

90 *winkered mule* — mule with blinkers.

90 *Belmullet* — a peninsula on the Mayo coast.

91 *Ha'p'orth* — a halfpenny's worth. A halfpenny was the smallest coin in general use.

91 *skelping* — thrashing, beating.

91 *hooshing him on* — lifting up his spirits and urging him on.

91 *the bogs* — wet, spongy ground consisting chiefly of decayed moss and other vegetable matter.

92 *and he astride* — if he were astride.

93 *a gallon can* — can which would contain 8 pints (about 4½ litres) of liquid.

93 *the butt of my lug* — the lobe of my ear.

93 *parlatic* — paralytic.

93 *Is my visage astray?* — Does my face look peculiar?

93 *the union* — the Workhouse where the old and destitute found shelter often in hard conditions.

93 *a straightened waistcoat* — a straitjacket.

94 *Darlint boy* — darling boy.

94 *a bagpipes* — i.e. of the Irish variety.

94 *A flat and three-thorned blackthorn* — walking stick made from the blackthorn shrub.

95 *banns* — public notice, usually announced on three consecutive Sundays, given in Church of an intended marriage so that those who know of any impediment thereto may lodge their objection.

95 *townland* — area.

96 *when Good Friday's by* — good Catholics do not make love in Lent — the three weeks in spring up to and including Good Friday, the day of Crucifixion of Jesus Christ.

96 *Lady Helen of Troy* — Helen, wife of Menelaus, abducted by Paris to Troy which was the cause of the Trojan War. A woman of incomparable beauty.

97 *paters* — paternosters — the Lord's Prayer, especially when recited in Latin.

97 *burning candles* — a reference to the Catholic practice of burning a candle in thanksgiving to God.

97 *kegs* — small barrels.

98 *turnkey* — man in charge of the keys in a prison.

98 *like holy Joseph in the days gone by* — reference to Joseph of Arimathaea who took Christ's body and gave Him a proper burial.

99 *gallous* — fine, spirited.

99 *crusted* — encrusted.

100 *drift of heifers* — herd of young cows.

100 *plains of Meath* — more fertile lands of Midlands and S.E. Ireland, proverbial in the West for their wealth.

100 *bedizened* — dressed up in vulgar finery.

100 *Pharoah's ma* — Pharoah's mother. Pharoahs were Ancient Egyptian kings renowned for their wealth.

101 *Sneem* — in Kerry, noted for its fine cattle.

102 *slitted* — slit him in half.

103 *slate* — beat unmercifully.

103 *saving only* — except.

104 *the old hen* — influenza.

104 *cholera morbus* — disease causing vomiting and cramp.

104 *the heaths of Keel* — area on Achill island, a short way to the south of Mayo. Lynchehaun found shelter on Achill.

104 *pandied* — beaten like a schoolboy.

105 *I'll stretch you first* — I'll lay you out (i.e. kill you) first.

108 *lighted sod* — piece of burning turf.

109 *limbo* — region on the border of Hell.

110 *picking cockles* — gathering these edible molluscs was the coldest, wettest and most badly paid work.

110 *stewing my oatmeal and washing my spuds* — porridge and potatoes — the basic diet of the poorest peasants.

111 *Putting her shawl over her head etc.* — i.e. traditional attitude of a woman lamenting the dead.

Donal Donnelly as Christy and Siobhan McKenna as Pegeen in a 1960 West End revival. (Photo: British Theatre Association)